Robert Caldwell, Nehemiah Goreh, Krishna Mohan Banerjea

Christianity Explained to a Hindu

Robert Caldwell, Nehemiah Goreh, Krishna Mohan Banerjea

Christianity Explained to a Hindu

ISBN/EAN: 9783743382831

Manufactured in Europe, USA, Canada, Australia, Japa

Cover: Foto ©Lupo / pixelio.de

Manufactured and distributed by brebook publishing software
(www.brebook.com)

Robert Caldwell, Nehemiah Goreh, Krishna Mohan Banerjea

Christianity Explained to a Hindu

CHRISTIANITY

EXPLAINED TO A HINDU:

OR

CHRISTIANITY AND HINDUISM COMPARED.

PILED FROM BISHOP CALDWELL, THE REV. NEHEMIAH GOREH, DR. KRISHNA MOHUN BANERJEA, AND OTHER WRITERS.

" Prove all things: hold fast that which is good."
The Bible.

SECOND EDITION, 3,000—TOTAL COPIES, 5,000.

\\\\\\\\\\\\\

MADRAS:

THE CHRISTIAN LITERATURE SOCIETY.

S. P. C. K. PRESS, VEPERY, MADRAS.

1893.

CONTENTS.

CHRISTIANITY EXPLAINED TO A HINDU:

OR,

THE DOCTRINES OF CHRISTIANITY AND HINDUISM COMPARED.

INTRODUCTION.

Almost every person in India has heard of the Christian religion. It is the professed creed of the rulers of the country, and of all enlightened nations throughout the world. More persons belong to it than to any other religion. Its nature is, therefore, deserving of inquiry. This is the more necessary as many erroneous opinions with regard to it are entertained by Hindus. It must also be acknowledged, with shame, that most persons who are called Christians give, by their conduct, a very incorrect idea of the religion they profess. It is desirable to know what Christianity really is. This will be explained by showing some of the most important points in which Christianity and Hinduism agree and differ.

Importance of Religion.—With regard to this, Christians and Hindus are of one opinion. Our stay in this world is short and uncertain. When we rise in the morning we can never tell whether before its close our remains will not be taken to the burning ground or laid in the grave. Alone we entered the world, and alone we depart. What is a man profited if he gain the whole world and lose his own soul? Religion concerns our happiness or misery in the next world when we must leave this, and enter upon an eternal state of being. Religion, therefore, is of infinite importance. Hinduism teaches that our daily life should be pervaded by it. Christianity does the same. Whether we eat or drink or whatever we do, should be done in obedience to God's commands.

Different Religions not roads to the same City.—It is a common idea in this country that all religions lead their followers to heaven. The folly of such an opinion can be seen by applying it to ordinary life.

Suppose a person is asking the road to a city. One man tells him to go north, another south, a third east, a fourth west: would they all lead him to the same place? At Allahabad several lines of railways meet, one going to Calcutta, another to Agra, &c., Suppose a traveller were in doubt which line to take, and some one said to him, "Go into any train; all are roads leading to the same city," what would you think of his reasoning?

It is just as false to say that all religions lead to heaven. If one be right, the others must be wrong.

"Every one should follow his own religion."—This is another common saying equally erroneous. There are many false religions in the world, some of them enjoining the most wicked practices. The Vamacharis commit nameless abominations; the Thugs strangled travellers in the name of the goddess Kali. According to the above maxim, religions—however false and however wicked their rites—should not be given up by those who hold them.

One God created all men, and His religion is one. All other religions are the inventions of men, and displeasing in His sight.

True Religion Needed.—Suppose a cooly, after labouring all day, were paid with bad money. When he went to the bazaar in the evening to buy food for his hungry and weary body, what he offered in payment would be refused as worthless. Suppose a man sold all his property to buy what he believed to be a precious diamond. If it turned out to be merely a piece of glass, he would have lost all in vain. So it is with religion. Unless it is the true one, it will profit us nothing.

Duty of Religious Inquiry.—In money matters people act wisely When a clerk receives his salary, he counts the rupees, and sees that they are all good. Even a woman when she goes to the bazaar to buy an earthen pot, taps it to find if it is sound, before she gives the money. In religion, however, people generally act like a flock of sheep, which, if the first leap over a bridge, the rest follow and are drowned.

Bad money may be known from good by means of the touch stone. God has given us a touchstone to distinguish between true and false religion—our reason. If we do not use it, we must suffer, like those men who take bad rupees without examination.

Differences as well as agreements to be considered.—A monkey and a man have each one head, one mouth, one tongue, two eyes &c.; but there are also essential differences between them. A dish of food may be composed of wholesome articles; but one kind of poison added to it would cause death to any one partaking of it So it cannot be said that Hinduism and Christianity are the same because they agree on some points. There are also irreconcileable differences between them. They cannot both be true. Even one great error, like the poison in food, may render a man's religio worthless.

Prayer for Light.—While it is our duty earnestly to inquir which is the true religion, we should ask for God's help to assist u in the search. Say to Him:

O all-wise, all-merciful God and Father, pour the bright beams c Thy light into my soul, and guide me into Thy eternal truth.

A REVELATION NEEDED AND GIVEN.

Hindus and Christians agree that a Revelation is needed, and that God has made known His will to men. Hindus have their Vedas, Puranas, and other Sastras; Christians have the Bible.

The Hindu Sastras are so numerous and differ so much, that all the views expressed in them cannot be noticed. Only the most important doctrines will be considered and compared with those in the Bible.

The claims of each to be regarded as the true Revelation will be better understood when their teachings have been contrasted.

GOD.

There is no more important question for a nation than this—What is the nature of the God it worships? *Yatha devah tatha bhaktah;* as is the God, so is the worshipper. We become like in character to the God we worship. If he is revengeful and impure, our evil passions will be strengthened; if He is loving and holy, we shall put on more and more of His image.

Right views about God lie at the foundation of true religion. Our welfare both in this world and the next depends upon Him. If we do what is displeasing in His sight, all our religious services will be in vain.

Important questions under this head will now be considered.

The Number of Gods.

There are three different opinions on this point. One is called *pantheism* (*pan,* all, *theos,* God), that all is God. Hinduism expresses it in the words *Ekamevādwitīyam,* "One only, without a second." This does not mean that there is only one God, but that nothing else exists. The Chhandogya Upanishad says, *Sarvan khalvidam Brahma,* "All this (universe) is Brahma."

The second opinion is called *polytheism* (*polus,* many, *theos,* God), a belief in many gods. In India this opinion is generally held along with pantheism. Ask any villager how many gods there are, and he will say, "There is only one God." At the same time he acknowledges the existence of 33 crores of divinities, including Brahma, Vishnu, Siva, with their wives and children.

The third opinion is called *monotheism* (*monos,* alone, one, *theos,* God), a belief in only one God, who is distinct from the universe which He has created. This is the doctrine of the Bible; in the Sastras the unity of God generally means pantheism.

In addition to those holding the above doctrines, there are two classes of unbelievers. An *atheist* (*a,* without, not, *theos,* God) is one who denies the existence of God. An *agnostic* (*a,* without, *gnosis,* knowledge) professes not to know whether there is a God or not, and, as a rule, does not care.

The three opinions first mentioned will now be briefly considered.

Pantheism.—The *mahavakya,* or great sentence of Vedantism, is *Tat twam asi,* "That art Thou," or *Aham Brahmasmi,* "I am Brahma." For a sinful, miserable mortal to use such language is blasphemy. We are as different from God as light is from darkness.

If a man is Brahma, so is a dog, a cat, a pig, a mosquito. If all this universe is Brahma, then it must be held that Brahma commits sin, that he steals, tells lies, and is guilty of murder, for men do such things. God is made the author of all sin, and so He must be a being infinitely worse, instead of infinitely better, than ourselves.

It is true that God is everywhere; but that is quite different from saying that God *is* everything. If it is held that Brahma and the world are the same, then there is no difference between the creator and the creature, between the potter and the pots he makes.

Our consciousness assures us that we are personal beings, different from everything around us and from our Creator. We also feel a personal responsibility for our actions.

Brahma is said to be *akhand,* indivisible : how then can he be divided ?

A Hindu writer justly says :

" The word *tat* (it) stands for the ocean of immortality, full of supreme felicity. The word *twam* (thou) stands for a miserable person, distracted through fear of the world. The two cannot therefore be one. They are substantially different. He is to be worshipped by the whole world : thou art but his slave."

Pantheism strikes at the root of all religious feeling. The essence of religion is to love, honour, and obey God, to pray to Him, to worship Him. If I am God, why should I worship myself ?

Pantheists in India look upon the popular deities as mere fictions of the popular mind. Their association with polytheism, says Flint, "means a conscious alliance with falsehood, the deliberate propagation of lies, a persisting career of hypocrisy. Pantheism, instead of elevating and purifying Hindu polytheism, has contributed to increase the number, the absurdity, and the foulness of its superstitions."

Polytheism.—Men are apt to judge of God by themselves. A king cannot be everywhere at the same time and attend to all the affairs of state. He has, therefore, many officers, each with his special duties. But God is everywhere and has all power. He does not require help. In any place and at any time, He is present to listen to our petitions. Inferior gods are not needed.

Hinduism professes to have 33 crores of gods and goddesses. The Chinese have about as many. They have a separate god for every disease and for every part of the body. They have goddesses who profess to teach a child to suck, to smile, &c. The folly of this is apparent.

It is sometimes said that all the gods are the same, though worshipped under different names.

Take the three principal gods, Brahma, Vishnu, and Siva. Their residences, wives, and children are all different. Brahma is said to live in Satya-loka, his wife is Savitri; Vishnu lives in Vaikuntha, his wife is Lakshmi; Siva lives in Kailasa, his wife is said to be Parvati. Different dispositions and actions are ascribed to these gods. Several times they are said to have fought with each other.

If the 33 crores of the Hindu gods are all the same, it may as well be said that the 25 crores of people in India with different houses, wives, children, occupations, are all one. If the gods are one, why are they reckoned as amounting to 33 crores?

This is only an excuse for the folly of polytheism put forward by those who are somewhat more intelligent than the masses. Rammohun Roy says: "The Hindus firmly believe in the real existence of innumerable gods and goddesses who possess in their own departments full and independent powers, and to propitiate them, and not the true God, are temples erected and ceremonies performed."

Bishop Caldwell says: "The Hindus themselves call their religions by the name of the particular deity they worship, as *Siva Bhakti, Vishnu Bhakti,* &c. The vast majority would be indignant at the supposition that their own religions, and the detested heresy of their opponents, are after all the same."

Monotheism.—As already explained, monotheism is a belief in only one God. It differs from pantheism in holding that He is distinct from the universe which He has created. God has existed from eternity, possessing all power and wisdom, infinite in justice, goodness, and holiness. There is no need of any other God. Christians, Muhammadans, and all enlightened nations now believe that there is only one God. Even Hindus admit this, although they combine with it pantheism and polytheism.

Which doctrine most honours God? which is most agreeable to reason?

Sin of Polytheism.—The Queen of England rules over about one-fifth of the earth's surface, and over more than 30 crores of its inhabitants. Throughout all her dominions, it is considered an act of high treason to set up any other sovereign than herself. Such a rebellion would at once be suppressed, and all who took part in it would be punished. People are not at liberty to set up any king they please. It is the same in every well-regulated state. Any other course would be fatal to the welfare of its people.

The British Empire is a very faint emblem of the vast dominions of the great Lord of all. The universe belongs to Him by creation. He spread the heaven above us. He formed the earth beneath us. He is the maker of all things visible and invisible. He first called us into existence. Asleep or awake, we are dependent upon Him for every breath that we draw. It is He who makes the rain to fall and the sun to shine. All that we have is His gift.

The nature of God's laws is an additional reason for obedience. His commands are "Holy, just, and good." He enjoins only what is best for ourselves; He prohibits only that which it is our highest wisdom to shun. Our duty and our happiness coincide.

Just as the Queen of England forbids any one from setting himself up as king within her empire, so does God forbid the worship of any other than Himself. This is His first command. He cannot permit the creatures whom He made to rise in rebellion against Himself.

God is both our Father and our King.

The worship of any other is a defiance of God's authority, a declaration that we will not have Him to rule over us. All the guilt that lies in foul rebellion against the mildest and most merciful of earthly monarchs—in disobeying the kindest and grieving the best of fathers, in ingratitude to a generous benefactor; all this evil, multiplied a thousand times, there is in polytheism.

THE CHARACTER OF GOD.

According to Hinduism, Brahm, the eternal supreme Being, in his ordinary condition, is *nirguna*, unfettered by action, or without qualities. A hot climate makes labour irksome, and gives an inclination to sleep. Brahm is also said to be *nishkriya*, inactive. He is represented as existing in a state of dreamless slumber: He is said to be *sat, cit, ananda*. He is pure unconscious Existence (*sat*); he is pure Thought (*cit*) with nothing to think about; he is pure Joy (*ananda*) with nothing to be joyful about, and only in the sense of being free from the miseries of transmigration.

The *nirguna* Brahm is a being without love or mercy. He neither sees, nor hears, nor knows, nor cares about any of his creatures; he has neither the power nor the will to do good or evil,—to reward the righteous, or punish the wicked. He is supposed to be like an Indian raja who spends his life in sloth, within his palace, heedless of what is going on throughout his dominions, and leaving everything to his ministers. The more a Hindu is like Brahm, the more selfish will he be, and the less profitable to all around him.

The God of the Bible is, in many respect a perfect contrast to

Brahm. He has, indeed, existed from all eternity. "From everlasting to everlasting Thou art God." But He is never unconscious;
He never slumbers nor sleeps. The care of the universe which He
called into existence is no burden to Him. "The Creator of the
ends of the earth fainteth not, neither is weary." He knows every
thing that takes place throughout His vast dominions. Not a hair
of our head can fall to the ground without His knowledge; every
thought of our heart is known to Him. His ear is ever open to
the cry of His children.

But Brahm does not always continue in this state of dreamless
repose. After the lapse of unnumbered ages, he awakes. Becoming conscious of his own existence, and dissatisfied with his own
solitariness, a desire for duality arises in his mind. Though himself *nirákár*, without form, he, in sport, imagines a form. How
desire arises in this unconscious being is a question which never
has been answered.

It is asserted that Brahm is *nirvikara*, incapable of change.
How is this statement consistent with the other statement that he
exists alternately in a *saguna* and a *nirguna* state? How can he
who is essentially immutable become sometimes void of qualities
and sometimes endued with qualities?

The three qualities which Brahm, in his *saguna* state, possesses
are *sattva*, truth, *rajas*, passion, a longing for worldly pleasure, and
tamas, darkness.

Prablada is represented, in the Vishnu Purana, as thus address-
ing Vishnu: "Thou art knowledge and ignorance, truth and falsehood, poison and ambrosia."

Brahma, Vishnu, and Siva are nowhere regarded in the Sastras
as holy beings. On the contrary, they are all described as stained
with great crimes. The way in which Brahma is said to have taken
five heads is too filthy to be described. Brahma, Vishnu, and Siva
are said to have been changed into children for their misconduct
with Atri's wife. To break the austerities of the wife of Brigu,
Vishnu cut off her head. Brigu consequently cursed him to seven
births among mortals. The conduct of Vishnu as Krishna, is well
known. Siva is said to have been notorious for his drunkenness
and love of bhang. He was ready to part with all the merit he
had acquired by his austerities in order to gratify his evil desires
but once with Mohini.

Power is the great attribute worshipped by Hindus. Just as
wicked and cruel despots are feared and honoured, so gods and
demons are worshipped whatever may be their character, provided
they will refrain from injuring or will confer some benefit on their
devotees. The gods of Hinduism act like Indian rajas, contending
with each other for power, each favouring his own party, and
indulging in every vice or committing any crime his evil heart
may desire.

The excuse is made, *Samarthi ko dosh nahin*, To the mighty is no sin.

The idea is taken from a Hindu despot, who could do anything he liked, such as take the wives of his subjects or put them to death without trial, no one daring to find fault. This was the usual character of their sovereigns, and when the Hindus manufactured gods they took them as a model. Their gods are deified men.

The principle that the gods are not to be condemned for wrong-doing is the opposite of the truth. If a child commit a fault, he is blamed ; if an ordinary man do the same, his guilt is greater ; if a king does it, the guilt and evil consequences would be still greater. Krishna himself says in the Bhagavad Gita : " Whatever the most excellent practise, other men practise likewise ; the world follows whatever example they set." Krishna's own example, as related in the Bhagavat Purana, has had a most pernicious effect upon his worshippers.

To say that the gods committed sin " in sport " or as a " divine amusement" only makes matters worse. Such an idea is blasphemous.

The Christian idea of God is very different. He is a God of truth. The Bible says, God is light and in Him is no darkness at all. His most glorious attribute is His spotless holiness. Sin is that abominable thing which He hates. "Holy, holy, holy is the Lord God of hosts." Instead of exhibiting, like Brahm, an example of selfishness, He is continually doing good to His creatures ; His character is expressed in one word—God is LOVE. Still, it is not the feeling which looks upon good and evil with equal eye. If a king allowed crime to be unpunished, his kingdom would become like a hell. But God's own declaration is, " As I live, saith the Lord God, I have no pleasure in the death of the wicked ; but that the wicked turn from his evil way and live."

A worshipper becomes like his God in character. It has been shown that the more a man resembles Brahm the more selfish and useless does he become. Would it be right for a man to copy some of the acts of Brahma, Vishnu, Siva, and Krishna ? On the other hand, the highest attainment of a Christian is to be pure, loving, and holy like God.

Which of the above views is the more reasonable ? which gives the more exalted idea of God ? It is plain that the 33 crores of Hindu divinities have no existence.

IDOLATRY.

Idolatry is the worship of God through images. Savages usually worship a stone or some object in its natural condition. Nations, half civilised, generally have images. The change from a stone to an idol may be very slight. A few chips or daubs of paint suffice to change the rude block into an idol.

In the Vedas idols do not seem to be mentioned ; but now it may be said of India, "the land is full of idols." They are found in nearly every Hindu dwelling.

On the other hand, idolatry is strongly condemned in the Bible. The first of the Ten Commandments forbids the worship of any other than one true God ; the second forbids the worship of images of every kind.

Hindus admit that Brahm is *nirákár*, without form. Christians say that God is a spirit. A sculptor may make an image of a man's body ; but can he make a representation of his soul ? It is equally impossible to make an idol like God. "To whom will ye liken me or shall I be equal ?" saith the Holy One.

Various excuses are made for idolatry.

Some say that idols are only like photographs, recalling friends to memory. To this it has been well replied :

"It is true that we like to retain photographs of people we love to remind us of their forms and features ; but of what sort of Divinity do blocks of stone or hideous images bought in the bazaar remind us ?"

If a son kept an image of a pig to remind him of his father, would this be right ? would the father be pleased ? It is infinitely worse to make an image of God.

But it is not true to say that idols are only to remind men of God. When a Hindu buys an idol or gets one made, he has the *pran pratishtha* ceremony performed, by which he believes that its nature is changed, and that it acquires not only life, but supernatural powers.

Statues of great men and women are often made by Europeans ; but there is no *pran pratishtha* ceremony, nor are they worshipped.

Another excuse is that idolatry is allowable for the ignorant.

To this it is replied, how is it that every Muhammadan in Turkey and every Protestant Christian from the highest to the lowest, can worship God without images ? The ignorant do not need images to remind them of God. They cannot understand His form for He has none. They can remember their parents when far distant ; they can love a benefactor whom they have never seen ; they can obey the authority of a Queen-Empress though she never set foot on their soil. They can worship God who is a Spirit in spirit and in truth. Idols are a hindrance, not a help, to true worship. They give most degrading ideas of God.

Folly of Idolatry.—Idolatry has been well compared to child's play. Little children talk to their dolls as if they had life. They dress them, pretend to give them food, put them to sleep, and so forth. Grown up people do just the same. They treat their idols as living beings. They offer them food, though they cannot eat ;

B

they have different kinds of music before images that cannot hear ; they have lights before what cannot see. In the cold season they furnish them with warm clothes ; in the hot season they fan them ; and lest mosquitoes should bite them, they place them within curtains at night.

Instead of the idols taking care of their worshippers, it is the latter who have to protect the former. They are constantly afraid lest the hands and feet of their gods should be broken. Robbers sometimes break into temples, and carry off the jewels. The gods cannot give even one good screech for help. Cockroaches sometimes destroy the colour of images ; rats make holes in them ; bats defile them ; flies, after sitting upon various unclean things, alight on them. Where is their divinity, seeing they suffer themselves to be thus insulted ?

Degrading Effects of Idolatry.—Krishna says in the Bhagavad Gita : " The mind by continually meditating on a material object becomes materialized." People who worship senseless images end by becoming like them. They are deceived and cheated by their religious teachers in every possible way ; but they do not see through the fraud.

God is self-existent, unchangeable, infinite in power, wisdom, goodness, and mercy, spotless in holiness. Who are worshipped in His stead ? Senseless blocks, blind, deaf, and dumb beasts, birds, and creeping things, the obscene linga, and supposed deities stained with every vice.

God's first command is not to worship any other than Himself. His second forbids the worship of idols.

Educated Hindus and Idolatry.—Many educated Hindus take part in idolatrous rites, pretending that they are harmless customs, kept up by female influence, and that they conform to them simply to avoid giving offence.

A leading Calcutta Native journal commended an Indian on his return from England for " good-naturedly obeying the requirements of Hinduism."

That idolatry is the very opposite of a " harmless custom" has already been shown. As well might a man be " good-naturedly" guilty of high treason against his sovereign.

The desire to please parents and relatives, within proper limits, is a praiseworthy feeling ; but to break God's first and great command at the wish of any human being is a plea which cannot be sustained for a moment. Suppose a parallel case. Parents urge a son to take part in a robbery ; they will be vexed if he does not consent. Would a judge accept such an excuse ? Would it be true kindness to his parents to join them in such an act ? Is he not rather bound, not only to abstain entirely from any participation in the crime, but to do his utmost to dissuade his parents from engaging in it ? It would be great cruelty to behave otherwise.

An intelligent educated man countenancing idolatry is guilty in the following respects :

1. *Of cowardly hypocrisy.*—Insincere and faithless observance of the rites of religion *must* be degrading and destructive to everything that is best and noblest in human nature. Religion is thus made a huge hypocrisy, from the want of courage and honesty.

2. *Of cruelty to his relations and countrymen.*

Women are the chief supporters of idolatry in India. Poor creatures they do not know better. Those who are mainly responsible for it and to be blamed are the educated men, who by their example encourage them in error. The women of India are naturally both intelligent and affectionate. If their husbands, instead of behaving as at present, would lovingly teach them to worship their great Father in heaven instead of idols, the reign of superstition would soon come to an end. The change is so reasonable as easily to be understood. It is so simple that it may be made intelligible even to a child.

3. *Of high treason against God.*

CREATION.

Creation means calling things into existence out of nothing. In this sense of the word, according to Hinduism there is no creation. Its fixed dogma is *navastuno vastusiddhih*, nothing can be produced out of nothing. God is indeed called *Sarva-karta*, maker of all ; but this does not mean that He is the *Creator*. No Hindu sect believes God to have created anything. Bramhos believe in a Creator, but they learned it from Christianity.

The Hindu doctrine is that every *Karya*, effect, must have an *Upadana Karana*, a cause out of which an effect is produced, such as clay is to an earthen pot. According to the Nyaya School, the *paramanus*, the atoms of earth, water, fire, and air, gods, animals, and plants are all uncreated, self-existent, and eternal. According to the Sankya system, *prakriti* is the material cause of the universe, and is, of course, self-existent and eternal. Even Maya, though false, is said to be eternal.

All that Brahma does after every successive dissolution (*pralaya*) is to *form* the world into its present shape. Hence he is called *Vidhata*, Arranger. Why does he do this ? Only to amuse himself ! Another explanation compares God to a gigantic spider who *evolves* the world out of his own substance, as a spider does its net. *Emanation* (a flowing from), not *creation* is supposed to be the true principle of the universe.

This illustration, false and blasphemous as applied to the great Creator, is the exact truth with regard to many Hindu speculations. Their authors evolved their deities, their philosophies, their astronomy, and geography, out of their own heads. They may be well compared to spiders' webs, unsubstantial, fitted to catch flies, but unable to sustain the pressure of human life.

The Christian doctrine, on the other hand, is that God, infinite in power and wisdom, has always existed, and that the universe and all that it contains was called into being by Him out of nothing.

The fundamental error of Hinduism is to judge God by our own standard. A carpenter cannot work without materials; in like manner it is supposed that God must have formed all things from eternally existing matter.

God is often called *Sarvashakti*, that is Almighty, in Hindu books, but this is not true in the proper sense of the word.

"Ye do err, not knowing the power of God" applies to Hindus as well as those to whom the words were addressed by the great Teacher.

Whether is it more rational to suppose the eternal existence of one Being, the Creator of all things by His omnipotent power, or to imagine that innumerable unintelligent atoms, gods, spirits, animals, and plants have existed from all eternity? Besides the latter, an eternal intelligent arranger is also required.

MAYA.

The doctrine of Maya is one great difference between Christianity and Hinduism. According to Vedantism, it is only through *Maya*, or illusion, that we look upon things as different and really existing. We are supposed to be like men who dream, to whom all things appear real so long as they dream. Christianity, on the other hand, affirms the reality of the universe, and the trustworthiness of our senses.

The following are some of the arguments against Maya:

1. *The Testimony of our Senses.*—Every one of our five senses —sight, hearing, taste, smell, and touch—bears witness to the reality of the objects around us.

The reply to this is as follows: A man sees a rope and by misapprehension takes it for a snake: in like manner the ignorant see the world, and suppose it to be real.

A man may, indeed, by misapprehension take a rope for a snake, but only so long as he keeps at a distance from it. Let him come near it, and he will at once see his error.

Another illustration is that the eye is deceived in mirage, fancying water to exist where there is none.

It is true that one sense may mislead us for a time, but the wrong idea is soon corrected by the other senses. The illusion of the mirage is detected by the touch. Kanada has well said, that it is only when the senses are unsound or defective or when some bad habit is contracted, that a person may be deceived.

According to Gotama: "If all evidence is to be rejected, then the refutation itself is inadmissible." The fact concerning the mirage is communicated to us through the senses. If the senses are never to be trusted, then how do we know about the mirage?

2. *The doctrine of Maya is incapable of proof.*—If all human beings are under the influence of the " eternal *Maya*," who is to find out that they are all deluded? How did the Vedantic philosophers discover it? Are they conscious of such an influence? But, on the supposition of the reign of universal and eternal delusion, is not that consciousness itself delusive? If it be said that the fact has been discovered by divine revelation; must not the perception of that revelation, as well as the comprehension of its import, on the supposition of a universal and eternal delusion, be also delusive?

3. *If the whole world is Unreal, the Vedas are also Unreal.*—The same applies to the Upanishads and all Vedantic writings.

4. *The doctrine gives a most dishonouring idea of God.*—" According to Vedantism, it is Brahma who has put the whole human race under the universal influence of the eternal *Maya*." He has projected a distorted reflection of himself with a view to delude his rational creatures. In consequence of this act he is termed *Mayavi Brahma !* How unworthy is such an opinion of the spotless and infinitely pure God ! Can it be conceived for a moment that He delights in deceiving mankind? Can the idea be entertained in the mind that the holy God, is, like a potent juggler, perpetually deceiving the whole human race as a " divine amusement ?"

The doctrine of Maya is pure imagination, utterly opposed to common sense. It has been well said of Hindu pandits, that the more a doctrine is opposed to common sense, the more they cling to it. Cicero, a distinguished Roman, said that there is no opinion, however absurd, which has not been held by some philosopher.

The doctrine of Maya is a good example of the spider-web theories of Hinduism.

ADRISHTA OR KARMA.

As Hinduism denies the *Creation* of the world in the strict sense of the word, so it denies its *Government* by God. All things are supposed to be determined by an irresistible power, called *Adrishta*, unseen, because felt and not seen. It stands for fate, merit or demerit on works during a previous state of existence. *Karma*, more commonly used, has the same meaning. It comes from *kri*, to do ; it means deeds or actions. According to *Karma* every action must bring forth its legitimate fruit. Sankar Acharya says, even God cannot alter it any more than He can produce rice out of wheat seed.

The doctrine of *Karma* has been adopted by Hindus as the only explanation of the unequal distribution of happiness in this world, why some are rich and others poor ; why some are healthy and others sickly.   If an infant agonise in pain, it arises from some great sin committed in a former birth.

The Hindu idea is that works *of themselves* produce their own fruits.   The Sankhya system unhesitatingly maintains that the performance of Hindu rites and ceremonies leads to happiness after death, while it denies that there is a God to reward them that diligently seek him.   Though most of the other systems acknowledge a God, *Ishwar,* he is only like a steward dispensing his master's goods according to his orders.   He has no choice in the matter, and the real master is the inevitable law which binds the action and its fruit together.   The real god of the Hindu, in the sense of the real master of his fate, is *Adrishta* or *Karma.*

On inquiry, however, it will be seen that this theory is attended with insuperable difficulties.

Adrishta, or *Karma,* is supposed to be endowed with most wonderful influence and qualities.   As a judge, its decisions are marked by unerring wisdom, and its awards are inevitably carried out to the letter.   They may be stated more in detail as follows :—

1.   *It is most wise.*—A judge of the High Court, able to sentence a man to death, needs great wisdom ; how much more is this necessary when the award may be heaven or hell for unnumbered ages ?

2.   *It is inflexibly just.*—A judge may be wise, but he may be partial.   Not so with *karma.*   It renders to every one exactly according to his deserts.

3.   *Its power extends to all worlds.*—Through it a person is born in one of 84 lakhs of births in this world, in the world of the gods, or in one of the hells.

4.   *It extends to all time.*—Its memory never fails.   A man may be in the enjoyment of happiness for millions of years on account of some supposed merit, but at the end of that period he may be born in the lowest hell for some crime in a former birth.

5.   *It is unalterable.*—The highest gods have no power to avert its effects ; they are themselves subject to *adrishta.*

6.   *Its object is good.*—To punish vice and reward virtue is an aim of the noblest kind.

What is it that Hindus suppose to possess these high attributes ? A mere name, something that has no existence.   What power is there in an action itself to reward or punish, millions of years after it was performed ?

As a rule, there must be some one to give the rewards or punishments due to men's actions.   Thus a man is engaged to do a certain work for which he is to receive wages.   The work done is the man's *karma :* the wages to be received is the *phala* or fruit.   But how is he to receive this *phala ?*   Is it to be received from the *karma ?* No. It must be given by some one able and willing to bestow it.   Suppose a thief steals many thousand rupees, will he be punished without the intervention of other persons ? Were any person to say that for the purpose of punishing the criminal no judge is necessary, that by demerit of the crime the man would be flogged without any one flogging him, would any person of common sense believe him ? And if such an assertion cannot be received as true respecting the affairs of this world, can similar assertions be received as true respecting the other world ?

There are other objections to the doctrine of *Karma*:

1. *It does not explain the origin of things.*—It only removes the difficulty one single step. Hindus have been obliged to go back from *Karma* to *Karma* until at last they have been forced to say that the world is eternal.

Before there could be merit or demerit, beings must have existed and acted. The first in order could no more have been produced by *karma* than a hen could be born from her own egg.

2. *The evil effects of a belief in Karma.*—Hindus consider that they are under the burden of a blind fate, which compels them to suffer for some crime or other of which they are unconscious. That punishment must be borne; they have no help for it; there is no way of escape as long as they live. Hence they are fatalists both in belief and practice.

In the Puranas persons guilty of the greatest crimes are comforted on the ground that all was fixed by their *karma*, that man has no power over that which is to be, and therefore they were not guilty of any fault. The excuse for misconduct is constantly made, " What could we do ? It was our *karma*."

The Christian view will now be explained.

God, the Ruler of the Universe.—It has been shown how absurd it is to suppose that a mere word can act the part of the wisest judge in millions of cases every day as is alleged to be done by *Karma*. On the other hand, all is agreeable to reason if, instead of *Karma*, we take God. He is eternal, the Creator of all things, having all power, inflexibly just, wise, and merciful. It is most fitting that He, the Lord of all, should be the Judge. This is what Christianity declares. His " dominion is an everlasting dominion and His kingdom is from generation to generation;" " He is Governor among the nations." He knows every thing. A holy man of old said : " Thou knowest my downsitting and mine uprising, Thou understandest my thoughts afar off. Thou compassest my path and lying down, and art acquainted with all my ways. For there is not a word in my tongue, but, lo, O Lord, Thou knowest it altogether." " Every one of us shall give an account of himself to God." " God shall bring every work into judgment, with every secret thing, whether it be good or whether it be evil." God " will render to every man according to his works."

Besides a judge to decide, an agency is necessary to carry out the sentence. While *Karma* has no power to do this, God is omnipotent; His power extends through all time and to every portion of the universe.

Hinduism denies free agency either on the part of God or man; Christianity affirms it in both. If we sin, it is our own fault.

MAN.

The Hindu idea is that all souls (*atma*) are exactly alike. Mind (*manas*) belongs not to the soul, but to the body. The human body has considerably more mind connected with it than the lower animals, but the difference is only one of degree.

Hindu speculations regarding the soul differ in several respects. On one point, however, they are nearly unanimous, that the soul is not created by God but eternal, *svayambhu*, self-existent.

The Kathavalli, says: "The wise one (that is the soul) is not born nor does he die; he has not come into existence from any cause, nor has any one (as something distinct from him) come into existence from him. He is unborn, eternal, permanent, the ancient; he is not killed when the body is killed."

On other points there are differences.

The Vaiseshika school maintains that the soul is diffused everywhere through space. "Ether, in consequence of its universal pervasion, is infinitely great; and so likewise is soul." VII. 22.

With this view the Bhagavad Gita agrees. The soul is described as "everlasting, all-pervading, stable, firm, and eternal."

On the contrary, the Svetasvatara Upanishad declares that the soul is almost infinitesimally small: "If the point of a hair be divided into one hundred parts, and each part again divided into one hundred parts—that is the length of the *atma*."

In the Katha Upanishad it is said that "Brahma, of the size of the thumb, dwells in the *atma*."

The Vedantic idea is that the soul is part of Brahm, and that to him it returns. A particle of him for a time is associated with a particle of Ignorance or Maya.

"The common people," says Dr. Kellogg, "speak of the soul as being 'a part of God.' It is a portion of the Supreme ruler as a spark is of fire. Yet in the same breath they will affirm that God is *akhand*, 'indivisible,' whence it follows that each soul is the total Divine Essence, and that is precisely the strict Vedantic doctrine! So one may go into any Hindu village and ask the first peasant that he meets who God is, and he will, to a certainty, receive the answer, *Jo bolta hai, wahi hai;* 'That which speaks, that same is He.'"

One argument for the eternity of the soul is the supposed axiom: "Whatever exists must always have existed." As already shown, this denies God's omnipotence. By His will He can create things or call them out of nothing into existence.

Another argument is that " Whatever had a beginning must have an end." This is also a denial of God's power. He can give a future eternal existence to any creature He has called into being. According to Hinduism, souls may pass into gods, demons, beasts, birds, reptiles, fishes, insects, into plants, and even into inanimate objects. Who can estimate the number of these eternal *svayambhu* essences ! Is it not perfectly unphilosophical, because absolutely unnecessary and egregiously extravagant, to assume such an indefinite numbers of eternal essences, when one Supreme Essence is sufficient to account for all things, visible or invisible, material or spiritual ?

If the soul is a portion of God, our relation to Him is that of whole and part. It is not necessary for God to worship Himself. If I am either God or a part of God, why should I worship Him ?

If a man denied the existence of his earthly parents, it would be a great sin ; but it is a much greater sin to deny that God is our Maker and Heavenly Father.

If our souls are eternal and self-existent, we are a sort of miniature gods. Our relation to God is changed. It is only that of king and subjects. His right over us is only that of might. It is only because He is mightier than we and of His possessing power to benefit and to harm us, that we should be anxious to pay homage to Him. There is not the love which a child should cherish towards a father. True religion is thus destroyed.

To any man endowed with a grain of common sense, the opinion maintained by some of the schools that the soul is infinite, like *akasa*, must seem the height of absurdity. Other views held are scarcely less extravagant, that it is eternal, *svayambhu*, self-existent.

The Christian doctrine is briefly as follows :—

God alone is self-existent, without beginning or end. He is omnipotent, able to call beings or things into existence out of nothing. He gave us a body and a soul. The soul never existed before our present birth. The body is mortal ; the soul returns to God who gave it. At the great day of judgment, all must appear before God, to answer for the deeds done in the body, whether good or evil.

As already mentioned, it is unphilosophic to maintain that there are innumerable self-existent beings, when one possessed of almighty power is sufficient. The explanation given by Christianity is beautifully simple and meets all the requirements of the case.

TRANSMIGRATION.

On account of its great importance, this famous Hindu dogma is noticed again, although some of its points have already been considered under *Karma*.

C

It is a fundamental doctrine of Hinduism that the "fruit of works" can be experienced *only in the body*, and therefore, as long as a man has an atom of merit or demerit unexhausted, he is bound to assume a fresh body. A South Indian poet thus expresses his feelings at the prospect:—

> "How many births are past, I cannot tell ;
> How many yet to come, no man can say ;
> But this alone I know, and know full well,
> That pain and grief embitter all the way."

The dread of continued transmigration is the one haunting thought with the Hindus. The great aim is, not to find truth or to be released from the burden of sin, but how to break this iron chain of repeated existences, how to return to complete absorption into pure unconscious spirit.

Transmigration, like *Karma*, is supposed to explain why some are born rich, others poor ; some healthy, others diseased, &c. All in this life, its feelings and actions, its joys and sorrows, its good and evil deeds, like fruit from a seed, are supposed to be the necessary result of actions performed in a former state of being.

This explanation is purely imaginary and destitute of proof ; while, on the other hand, there are several arguments showing that transmigration cannot be true.

1. *Like always produces like.*—Every animal, every plant produces animals and plants exactly like itself. According to transmigration, a man in his next birth may be a lion, a pig, an insect, or a pumpkin. The analogy of nature is a strong presumption against its truth.

2. *No one has the slightest recollection of any previous birth.*—It is the same soul that transmigrates. A traveller who journeys from city to city remembers his native place from which he started, the relations he left there ; he recollects, too, the different cities through which he passed, and what happened to himself in each. The body, we are told, is the "city of Brahma," and the soul as it enters new "cities" ought to carry with it a complete recollection of its past history. But no soul remembers anything that happened to it previous to its present life. The proof then is almost perfect that it never lived before.

3. *By transmigration persons virtually become new beings, so that they are in reality punished for the actions of others.*—It is said that at every new birth something takes place by which the remembrance of former things is destroyed. In this case the person on whom it is wrought is no longer the same person. The object of transmigration is to purify the soul by lessons of warning from its past history. This is lost when a person knows not what he did and why he is punished. Suppose a magistrate said to a peon, "Bring in that man and give him 50 lashes ;" would not the man ask, "Why am I flogged?" What would be thought of such a

magistrate? According to transmigration, one man is really punished for the faults of another of which he is quite ignorant.

4. *The doctrine tends to make people earthly-minded.*—The rewards of virtue are only to be enjoyed in bodily life. They are generally supposed to consist in riches, honour, rank, many children, long life, &c. The effect of such a view is to fix people's attention on earthly good things, and to make them regard virtue only as means to that end.

5. *Belief in transmigration weakens the inducements to virtue and encourages vice.*—It has been shown that the person who does the acts is neither rewarded or punished. The *phala* may not be reaped till after thousands of births. There is therefore no motive for me to conduct myself so as to obtain that enjoyment or avoid that suffering.

The doctrine tends to annul the office of conscience which God has appointed to shame and reproach us when we do wrong and to encourage us in what is right. The Hindu looks upon the blessings of this life as rewards for meritorious acts in some former state of existence. They are the payment of a just debt, for which no gratitude is due to God. If a man meets with misfortunes, he does not impute them to present misdeeds, for which he should repent, but to some sins in a former birth of which he is not conscious.

6. *Happiness does not depend merely on rank or wealth.*—It is generally supposed that a king is happy and a poor man miserable. Often the reverse is the case. There is much less inequality in the condition of men than people think. A king gets accustomed to rich food, and feels no more pleasure in eating it than a poor man when taking his dinner. The sleep of the poor man is sweet; the nights of the great are often troubled. Shakespeare says,

"Uneasy lies the head that wears a crown."

Kings are liable to be assassinated. They are tempted to many sins. An Indian proverb says, "The fruit of a kingdom is hell." Where is the blessing of a kingdom if such is its result?

7. *Happiness or Misery is often traceable to conduct in this life.*— The facts brought forward to prove a prior existence may be, in a great measure, accounted for by differences observable in the world itself, in the actions of men. One man prospers, not on account of his merit in a former birth, but through his industry; another is unfortunate, not from former demerit, but through his laziness. It is foolish to ascribe to *Karma* what is plainly the result of a man's own acts in this world.

8. *We may look forward as well as backward.*—The strongest argument for transmigration is that it seems to satisfy our sense of justice. This is also done by the Christian doctrine, which is that this world is a state of probation and trial, preparatory to a future state.

We are like the servants of a great king who has allotted to us different duties, and according as we discharge them we shall be dealt with. People are tested in different ways,—some by riches, some by poverty, some by health, some by sickness, some by prosperity, some by adversity. Happiness or misery depends far more upon ourselves than upon outward things.

Christians, instead of ascribing misfortunes to the consequences of a former birth, refer them either to what they have done in this life or regard them as God's fatherly dealings with them to purify them, just as their earthly parents corrected them to do them good.

Those who truly love and serve God may always be happy, and can meet even death with joy as a messenger calling them to their Father's house, there to dwell for ever. They have no dread, like Hindus, of unknown future births.

Caste and the Brotherhood of Man.

Caste is the distinguishing feature of Hinduism. A man may be an atheist, pantheist, polytheist, monotheist, he may be a liar, thief, adulterer, murderer; but so long as he observes caste he is recognised as a Hindu and has free admission to its temples. On the other hand, let him eat with a European, let him go to England for study, or marry a widow, and he is excluded from Hindu society. All beyond the pale of Hinduism are considered impure Mlechchas.

" The rigid observance of caste," says Rammohun Roy, " is considered in so high a light as to compensate for every moral defect. Even the most atrocious crimes weigh little or nothing in the balance against the supposed guilt of its violation. Murder, theft, perjury, though brought home to the party by a judicial sentence, so far from inducing a loss of caste, is visited with no peculiar mark of infamy or disgrace."

Caste has chiefly reference to food. Hence it has been said that the *stomach is the seat of Hinduism.*

" Other religions may be seated in the mind and soul—but the stronghold of Hinduism is the stomach. A Hindu may retain his faith against all argument, and against all violence, but mix a bit of beef in his food, and his religion is gone ! Not that he renounces it, but that it repudiates him. Let half a dozen Hindus seize one of their own caste, and forcibly thrust forbidden food down his throat, and that man has ceased to have any rights in this world or the next."

It is often alleged that caste distinctions are similar to the civil and social distinctions of European and other nations ; but there is an essential difference. Indian caste is derived from *birth* alone. It cannot be transferred from one class to another; it cannot be gained as a reward for the highest merit or bestowed as an honorary title by the most powerful monarch. As well might an ass be changed into a horse.

Civil distinctions in Europe were framed by man ; caste claims divine origin. Krishna, in the Bhagavad Gita, says : " The fourfold division of castes was created by me."

Origin of Caste.—The sacred books of the Hindus contain no consistent account of the origin of caste ; but, on the contrary, present the greatest varieties of speculation on the subject.

The most common story is that the castes issued from the mouth, arms, thighs, and feet of Brahma. The Satapatha Brahmana says that they sprung from the words *bhuh, bhuvah, svah.* The Taittiriya Brahmana says that they were produced from the Vedas. In another place the same book says the Brahman caste is sprung from the gods ; the Sudra from the asuras. In one book men are said to be the offspring of Vivasvat ; in another his son Manu is said to be their progenitor ; whilst in a third they are said to be descended from a female of the same name. The Bhagavata Purana says that in the Krita or Satya Yuga there was but one caste. The Vayu Purana says that the separation into castes did not take place till the Treta Yuga.

When witnesses in a court of justice give conflicting evidence, discredit is thrown upon all their testimony. Writings cannot be inspired which involve self-contradictions.

Caste first arose from difference of *race.* The ordinary names for caste prove thus. *Játi* means race ; *Varna,* colour.

The Aryas, coming from a colder climate, were lighter in colour than the original inhabitants of India, whom they called " the black skin."

The first great distinction was between the white and dark races, the conquerors and the conquered, the freeman and the slave. The Sudras undoubtedly were the aboriginal races of India subdued by the Aryan invaders. One of the earliest tribes brought under subjection was called *Sudras,* and this name was extended to the whole race.

Difference of *employment* was another cause. In every civilized country there are priests, soldiers, merchants, and men following other occupations. Manu represents the castes to have multiplied by marriages between the four original castes. These mixed castes did not wait for mixed marriages before they came into existence. Professions, trades, and handicrafts had grown up without any reference to caste. Some castes, as the musicians, called Vinas, from *vina,* the lyre, got their name from their occupations.

Difference of *place* was a third cause. Servants who waited on ladies were called Vaidehas, because they came from Videha.

Subdivisions of castes arose from jealousy between rival families, difference in religion, &c.

The following extracts from Manu's Code show that caste rules are an invention of the Brahmans to enslave all others :

Brahmans.

93. Since he sprang from the most excellent part, since he was the first-born, and since he holds the Vedas, the Brahman is, by right, the lord of all this creation.

100. Thus whatever exists in the universe is all the property of the Brahman ; for the Brahman is entitled to all by his superiority and eminence of birth. Book I.

Sudras.

413. But a Sudra, whether bought or not bought, (the Brahman) may compel to practise servitude ; for that (Sudra) was created by the Self-existent merely for the service of the Brahman.

417. A Brahman may take possession of the goods of a Sudra with perfect peace of mind, for, since nothing at all belongs to this (Sudra) as his own, he is one whose property may be taken away by his master. Book VIII.

281. If a low-born man, endeavours to sit down by the side of a high-born man, he should be banished after being branded on the hip, or (the king) may cause his backside to be cut off.   Book VIII.

80. One may not give advice to a Sudra, nor (give him) the remains (of food) or (of) butter that has been offered.   And one may not teach him the law or enjoin upon him (religious) observances.

81. For he who tells him the law and he who enjoins upon him (religious) observances, he indeed, together with that (Sudra), sinks into the darkness of the hell called Asamvrtta (unbounded.)   Book IV.

According to Manu, if a Sudra sat at a meeting of the National Congress in the presence of Brahmans, he should be banished after being branded or mutilated !

Manu's Code professes to have proceeded from the Self-existent. Let any intelligent Hindu say honestly whether some of the laws which have been quoted could have had such an origin.

Evils of Caste.—Caste is founded on a lie. Sir H. S. Maine, in *Ancient Law*, justly describes it as, "The most disastrous and blighting of human institutions."

Keshub Chunder Sen says in an "Appeal to Young India :"—

" That Hindu caste is a frightful social scourge no one can deny. It has completely and hopelessly wrecked social unity, harmony, and happiness, and for centuries it has opposed all social progress. But few seem to think that it is not so much as a social but as a religious institution that it has become the great scourge it really is. As a system of absurd social distinctions, it is certainly pernicious. But when we view it on moral grounds it appears as a scandal to conscience, and an insult to humanity, and all our moral ideas and sentiments rise to execrate it, and to demand its immediate extermination. Caste is the bulwark of Hindu idolatry and the safeguard of Brahminical priesthood. It is an audacious and sacreligious violation of God's law of human brotherhood. It makes civil distinctions inviolable divine institutions, and in the name of the Holy God sows perpetual discord and enmity among His children ! It exalts one section of the people above the rest, gives the former, under the seal of divine sanction, the monopoly of education, religion and all the advantages of social pre-eminence, and visits them with the arbitrary authority of exercising a tyrannical sway over unfortunate and helpless millions of human souls, trampling them under their feet and holding them in a state of miserable servitude. It sets up the Brahminical order as the very vice-gerents of the Deity and stamps the mass of the population as a degraded and unclean race, unworthy of manhood and unfit for heaven."

The " Brotherhood of Man" is now claimed as a Hindu doctrine. There is not much "brotherhood" when brothers regard it as pollution to eat with one another. The "Fatherhood of God" is also claimed as taught by Hinduism.. Amid the thousand or more names given to God in the Sastras, father is to be found; but this does not prove it, for the essential feature is wanting. A father is one through whom we receive life; but according to all Hindu sects souls are eternal and self-existent like God Himself.

On the other hand Christianity teaches that God gave us life, and continually preserves us. He is therefore our Father in heaven. We are all descended from the same first parents. Climate, exposure to the weather, and different modes of life have produced the differences, fitting persons to live in different countries. An English poet says :—

" Children we are all
Of one Great Father, in whatever clime
His providence hath cast the seed of life ;
All tongues, all colours."

The Brotherhood of Man follows from the Fatherhood of God. All people in the world should regard themselves as brothers and sisters of one great family, with God as their Father. It is true that they act very differently; but this arises from their sinfulness.

Mr. P. C. Mozoomdar makes the following admission : "The idea of the brotherhood and equality of all mankind before God, I am sorry to say, is not to be found, because it is never recognised in any of our ancient writings. The idea is decidedly foreign, Western, and I think I might say Christian."

Whether is the teaching of Hinduism or Christianity on this point the more consistent with truth and justice ? Well may the Hindus echo the prayer of the *Indu Prakash* :

"Oh God, have mercy on our fallen-countrymen! Give them true knowledge of Thy Fatherhood, and their brotherhood; that our countless millions may be bound by one social tie, and joining hand with hand, and heart with heart, move onward in the path of freedom and righteousness, knowledge and glory, and national regeneration."

MAN'S DUTY, OR THE AIM OF LIFE.

Hinduism makes life a curse instead of a blessing. The body is regarded as the mean lodging-place for vile worms and many diseases ; men suffer from their fellowmen, from famines, pestilences, from the malignant influence of evil stars, or from the cruelty of demons and hobgoblins. The great object is to cut short the 84 lakhs of births exposed to such calamities.

By the *Karma marga*, by ceremonies and virtuous deeds, the Hindu supposes that he may obtain happiness, but it is only temporary. The following illustration is used :—

"We are bound to our existence by two chains, the one a golden chain and the other an iron chain. The golden chain is virtue, and the iron chain is vice. We perform virtuous actions and we must exist in order to receive their reward ; we perform vicious actions, and we must exist in order to receive their punishment. The golden chain is pleasanter than the iron one, but both are fetters, and from both should we seek to free our spirit."

"We must seek a higher end—deliverance from pain and pleasure alike—and look for it by nobler means, by being free from works altogether. Knowledge is the instrument, meditation the means by which our spirit is to be freed. To avoid all contact with the world, to avoid distraction, to avoid works, and to meditate on the identity of the internal with the external spirit till their oneness be realised, is the 'way of salvation' prescribed by the higher Hinduism."

This is pure selfishness. The personal happiness of the individual is the only consideration. His aim is neither to see, hear, nor care about what goes on in the world around him. The people of his nation may be sunk in ignorance, he is not to instruct them ; they may be starving from famine, he is not to provide them with food ; they may be dying from pestilence, he is not to give them medicine. With his eyes fixed on the tip of his nose, he is to try to meditate without any object. He is to refrain from all actions, good or bad, till at last he blasphemously thinks that he is God.

Christianity, on the other hand, teaches us to make *God*—not *self* —the centre of our thoughts, the end of our existence.

A child should love, honour, and obey his earthly father ; a subject should respect his rightful king, render to him his just service, and obey his laws. God stands to us in both relations. To him we are indebted for existence; our parents were, as it were, only the instruments in His hand. He is our Father in heaven. One of the oldest names of God used by the Aryans before they entered India was *Dyaus Pitar*, Heaven-Father. From our birth to the present moment we have been dependent upon Him for every breath we draw ; every blessing we enjoy is His gift. We should regard Him as an affectionate child looks upon his father. But God is also

our sovereign. He is the rightful Lord of the universe which He has
created. His laws are holy, just, and good. To worship any other
than Himself, is rebellion. To ascribe to Him human vices, is to
be guilty of blasphemy.

A holy man of old says, " Praise the Lord, O my soul. While I
live I will praise the Lord. I will sing praises unto my God while
I have any being." According to Hindu philosophy, worship of
God is only a means of obtaining *jnana*. When it has been reached,
the worship of God ceases for ever. On the contrary, the longer
we exist, the more should we love and honour God, the more should
we desire to become pure and holy like Himself.

The first and great commandment of Christianity is to love God
with all our heart, and soul, and strength.

Again, a child should love his brothers and sisters, and always
treat them with justice and kindness. All men are children of the
same Heavenly Father, and they should behave towards each other
as brethren. We should do all the good we can to our fellow-men.

The second great commandment is, Thou shalt love thy neighbour
as thyself. It is also expressed in what is called the Golden Rule,
"All things whatsoever ye would that men should do to you, do
ye even so to them."

Our duty may be summed up in *love to God* and *love to man*.

While his own happiness is not the aim of the Christian, he takes
the surest way to promote it. He seeks it, not in himself, but
in God. God is an ocean of happiness, and the more we are like
Him, the more shall we be partakers of His joy.

SIN.

Distinction between Right and Wrong.—Hinduism denies the
reality of an eternal and necessary distinction between righteousness and sin. The difference is not inherent, but accidental.
The uncleanness or murder which is wrong in me may be right
for another person. In the Bhagavat Purana, the worshipper of
Krishna is told not to imitate the deeds to the accounts of which
he listens. According to the saying already quoted, " To the
mighty is no sin." As Brahma is the only real existence and
I am myself Brahma, it follows that sin and righteousness exist
only in my conceptions, and the distinction between them is only
imagined under the power of illusion. A song of South India says:

> " To them that fully know the heavenly truth,
>   There is no good or ill; nor anything
> To be desired, unclean or purely clean.
>
> Where God is seen, there can be nought but God,
>   His heart can have no place for fear or shame;
> For caste, uncleanness, hate, or wandering thought,
>   Impure or pure, are all alike to him."

D

As previously shown, in reality both sin and righteousness are alike evil, for the fruit of both must be reaped.

Christianity, on the other hand, affirms the eternal distinction between right and wrong.

It is admitted, however, that Hindus, in this respect, are better than their creed. Conscience, to some extent, convinces them of sin, and warns of punishment.

What Sin is.—Among most Hindus, breaking the rules of their caste is the chief sin. They believe that if they bathe every day, perform puja, repeat the names of their gods, feed Brahmans, and abstain from certain food, they are righteous, though they may lie, cheat, oppress the poor, and lead immoral lives.

The taking of animal life is among Hindus now considered one of the greatest sins. It was not always so. The Rishis who wrote the Vedas killed cows, and ate their flesh. Thus did Vasistha when entertaining Visvamitra, Janaka, and other sages. The present feeling was acquired from Buddhism. According to Hinduism, all life is the same—vegetable and animal. The one may pass into the other. Hence Brahmans are, by Manu, forbidden to cultivate; Buddhist priests should not even break off the leaf of a plant.

But any man who thinks seriously must acknowledge that breaking absurd caste rules is no sin, while actions that are thought lightly of are great sins. A man is defiled, not when he eats food prepared by a person of different caste, but when his mouth pours forth lies, angry or filthy words.

Sin is disobedience to God. God's nature is holy, and He commands only what is right. Sin consists in preferring our own sinful desires to God's will.

All know that to commit adultery is sin; but many do not consider that thoughts may be sinful as well as actions. Thoughts are the seeds of which actions are the fruit. Before a man commits murder, angry hateful thoughts arise in his mind. The great Teacher says that whoever looks upon a woman to lust after her, hath already committed adultery with her in his heart.

A son is disobedient if he does not do what his father tells him, as well as when he does what his father has forbidden. So we may sin in what we leave undone as well as in what we do.

A child should love, honour, and obey his parents. If he does not do so, he commits sin. God, who gave us life and keeps us in life, is our Father in heaven. It is our duty, above all, to love, honour, and obey Him. If we do not do so, we sin. Have we done so? Alas! no. We have forgotten Him, disobeyed His commands, which are holy, just, and good, and followed our own sinful desires.

Man Sinful.—It is generally allowed that man is a fallen being. His inclination to wrong-doing is such that all means employed to counteract it often prove fruitless. Bolts and bars are needed to protect property; bonds and deeds to check frauds; prisons, the lash, and the scaffold, to deter criminals. In a world of virtue such would have no place. Man, also, is born to trouble as the sparks fly upwards.

According to Hindu philosophy, what is the cause of man's debasement? *Agnana*, ignorance. By *agnana* is not meant ignorance of God, but ignorance of the identity between the soul and Brahm.

Christianity traces man's degradation to sin. He has broken God's laws, and he is suffering the consequences. All are guilty before God: "There is none righteous, no, not one."

There are some remarkable Hindu acknowledgments of man's sinfulness. The following confession ought to be repeated daily by Brahmans:

Pápoham pápakarmáham pápátmá pápasambhavah:

The meaning is: I am sin; I commit sin; my soul is sinful; I am conceived in sin.

A Hindu writer says, "This powerful devil of a deceitful heart is fiercer than fire, more impassable than the mountains, and harder than adamant: sooner might the ocean be emptied than the mind be restrained."

There are statements very similar in the Bible. David says. "Behold, I was shapen in iniquity; and in sin did my mother conceive me." It is also written: "The heart is deceitful above all things and desperately wicked; who can know it." It has been compared to the nim tree, always producing bitter leaves and fruit, until its nature has been changed.

We are born with a sinful nature. Our parents are sinful, and we inherit their disposition. "Who can bring a clean thing out of an unclean? Not one." This is shown by the conduct of mere infants. Before they are able to speak, they sometimes try to beat their mothers.

The holiest men are the first to admit their own sinfulness. Most people compare themselves with their neighbours, and are satisfied if they come up to their standard. Sometimes they contrast themselves with persons notoriously wicked, and are proud because they think themselves better. Truly good men compare themselves with what God's law requires, and their confessions "We are all as an unclean thing, and all our righteousnesses are as filthy rags."

The two great sins chargeable against every human being are *ungodliness* and *selfishness*.

The verdict pronounced upon Belshazzar, king of Babylon, was: "Thou art weighed in the balance, and art found wanting." The prophet Daniel explained the grounds of this judgment when he said, "The God in whose hand thy breath is, and whose are all thy ways, hast thou not glorified." When conscience awakes, we

see nothing in the past but a career of guilt—the grand purpose of
our lives neglected, the great God treated with indifference, His
holy law trampled under foot. God contrasts the gratitude of the
very beasts with the regardlessness of man. "I have nourished
and brought up children, and they have rebelled against me. The
ox knoweth his owner and the ass his master's crib; but Israel
doth not know, my people doth not consider."

Excuses for Sin.—The blame is often laid upon God or *karma*.
"We must do whatever Brahma has written on our heads." Men,
in their dealings with each other, do not accept such an excuse.
Does a thief get off because he said that Brahma had written on
his forehead that he was to steal ? We know that he was not forced
to steal, but did it of his own free will, and that he deserves to be
punished.

Suppose a wicked son laid the blame of his misconduct on his
wise and good father, saying that he had only done what he made
him do; would such an excuse be accepted ? It would be known to
be false, and, instead of lessening his guilt, would only increase it.
So it is a great sin to lay the blame of our bad actions upon God
who is of spotless holiness and abhors sin.

Our consciences tell us that our sins are our own, and not God's
or fate's.

PUNISHMENT OF SIN.

All admit that good conduct deserves approval, and that wrong-
doing should be followed by punishment. A just king bestows
honours on faithful servants, while he punishes those who break
his laws and are traitors against his Government. We should blame
a king who treated alike obedient subjects and open rebels. It
cannot be supposed that the great Creator and Lord of the universe
has a less sense of justice than some of His creatures. The belief
is therefore general that the good will be rewarded and the wicked
punished. This is the case, in some measure, even in this life, but
only to an imperfect extent. In another world, all will be rectified.

Future punishments, according to Hinduism, are explained in
Manu's Code, the Vishnu Purana, &c.

The following are some of them. Manu says:—

As many times as (are) the hairs on the beast, so many times in
the next world does one who in vain slaughters beasts obtain
a violent death from birth to birth. V. 38.

According to the Vishnu Purana, a horsedealer falls into the
Taptaloha (red-hot iron) hell. He who eats by himself sweetmeats
mixed with his food, and those who rear cats, cocks, goats, dogs,
hogs, or birds fall into the Puyavaha (where matter flows) hell.
Fishermen go to the Rudhirandha hell (whose wells are of blood).
Shepherds, hunters, and potters go to the hell called Vahnijwala

(or fiery flame). The student of religion who sleeps in the day, and adults who are instructed in religion by their children go to the Swabhojana hell where they eat dog's flesh. As numerous as are the offences that men commit, so many are the hells in which they are punished. Book II. Chap. 6.

Any intelligent man reading the foregoing will see that they are mere inventions. Why should a horsedealer fall into a red-hot iron hell?

It has been mentioned that some of the Hindu gods committed sin *in sport*; according to Christianity sin is the abominable thing which God hates. The Bible declares that the " wages of sin is death." This includes not only the death of the body, but punishing in hell.

Criminals on trial are not proper judges of the sentences which should be passed upon them. If left to their decision, the sentences would be very slight. In like manner we cannot form a right opinion as to the punishment our sins deserve.

God claims to be supreme over the world which He has created; it is essential to the welfare of the universe that He should be supreme. Every sin is a denial of His authority, a breach of his commands.

Suppose a man committed theft, the value of the article stolen has not simply to be considered. The evil is that if theft did not involve a penalty, no man's property would be safe. It is the same with sin. A single violation of God's law with impunity, would tend to spread rebellion through the universe.

According to Christianity, there are no future births. At death the condition of man is determined for ever. The righteous enjoy everlasting happiness; the wicked suffer everlasting misery.

Future punishments will differ. Some will be beaten with " many," some with " few stripes." What the exact nature of the punishment will be we do not know. Conscience will gnaw like an undying worm. Milton makes Satan say, " myself am hell."

Some think that the wicked will be purified in hell and afterwards received into heaven. Why do they think so? The tendency of punishment is rather to harden than to soften the heart. So long as men go on sinning, so long must they suffer.

But even according to Hinduism, sin involves intense suffering in various hells for countless ages. One great object should be to escape this terrible fate, to obtain, if possible, the pardon of sin.

PARDON OF SIN.

The feeling is universal, that man is a sinner, and that sin deserves punishment. The most momentous inquiry that can agitate the human breast is, How can I, a consciously guilty, sin-polluted being, be delivered from this load of evil, obtain forgiveness, and be restored to the Divine favour?

Why free Pardon impossible.—It may be said, that as an earthly parent forgives a repentant child, so we may be pardoned by our Heavenly Father. But a very important distinction has already been pointed out. God is our Sovereign as well as our Father. If a king were to pardon offenders upon their repentance, his laws would soon be disregarded, and his whole realm would be deluged with crime. And there are other reasons.

The relation in which God stands to His intelligent creatures is that of a moral Governor, who has given them a law—to the transgression of which He has attached the heaviest of penalties. What this law commands is eternally right; and what it forbids is eternally evil. Penalty, as attached to transgression, is not a mere expedient to deter men from committing it, and so to prevent the injury to His creatures which would result from its prevalence. First and foremost is penalty designed to mark sin as in itself vile and hateful, and to do homage to the eternal law that wrong-doing deserves to suffer.

Among people of all nations, there is a tendency to believe in the necessity of some atonement for sin. Can the instinct of almost the whole human race be wrong? Hinduism has always been full of self-made atonements.

Hindu ideas of the Pardon of sin.—These are contradictory. According to the doctrine of *karma* every sin must have its punishment : even Brahm cannot interfere with this law. On the other hand, it is taught that the greatest sins may be removed by the most inadequate means.

Some trust to almsgiving. It is our duty to assist the deserving poor, and God commands us to do it. But much of Hindu charity is given to able-bodied beggars, too lazy to work, and given up to vice. This is not true charity, but the encouragement of wickedness. In any case almsgiving will not atone for sin. If a thief is brought before a judge, will he be pardoned because he has given some pice to beggars?

Going on pilgrimages is another supposed way of obtaining pardon of sin. Instead of sin being thus decreased, it is increased. At great places of pilgrimage, sins are committed which the fear of discovery would prevent at home. Water may cleanse the body, but it cannot purify the soul. Pilgrimages neither atone for sin, nor make the heart holy.

Torturing the body, such as suspending one's self with the head downwards, sitting in circles of fire, &c., is practised by some to obtain the pardon of sin and acquire merit. Do these persons become holy? Pride is one of the greatest sins a creature can commit. When a sinner, by the help of God, becomes, in some measure, holy, he is filled with humility, because he knows that he has nothing to be proud of. What reason has a filthy, starving, and wretched beggar to be proud in the presence of a great king? What reason has sinful miserable man to be proud in the sight of a holy and glorious God? Yet persons who practise austerities are filled with pride. And not only so. It is notorious that many sanyasis are addicted to some of the worst vices.

Other modes of obtaining pardon, mentioned in the Sastras, are equally useless.

The Padma Purana says:

"He who carries in his body a drop of water in which a Brahman's toe has been washed, gets all his sins immediately destroyed."

The Mahabharat says:

"He who contemplates the Ganges, while walking, sitting, sleeping, thinking of other things, awake, eating, breathing, and conversing, is delivered from all sins."

The Bhagavat says that, "a person pronouncing loudly 'reverence to Hari,' even involuntarily, in the state of falling down, of slipping, of labouring under illness, or of sneezing, purifies himself from the foulest crimes."

The Vishnu Dharm Tantra says, "As without knowledge fire burns when anything touches it, so the name of Vishnu, even without knowledge, burns up all sins."

Hence the Hindus give their sons the names of their gods, under the idea that merit will be acquired even when calling them for any purpose. The story is told that Ajamila, who had killed cows and Brahmans and lived in the practice of evil all his days, was taken to heaven, because in the hour of death he called on his son Narayana to give him some water. The Kashi Khand tells of Guna Nidhi, who was taken to heaven because he had eaten some stolen food on the Siva Ratri, and had made a lamp burn brightly that he might see the food.

The Durga Nam Mahatmya says, "He who pronounces 'Durga,' though he constantly practise adultery, plunder others of their property, or commit the most heinous crimes, is freed from all sins."*

Among the heinous sins requiring *prayaschitta* is that of going to England. Giving a widowed daughter in marriage or marrying a widow are crimes equally great. The great means of purification is swallowing the five products of the cow, and giving presents to Brahmans. The last is indispensable, and will cover all sins, if sufficient in amount.

To any thoughtful man the inadequacy of the means for the removal of sin is apparent. It has been admitted by Hindus themselves. One writer says: "He whose heart is not pure will not be clean though he should get his body rubbed with mud as much as

* Quoted by Ram Mohun Roy. Works, Vol. I. p. 146.

would form a mountain, and bathe in the Ganges as long as his life would last."

Members of the Brahma Samaj have adopted from Christianity more correct views, in some respects, with regard to the pardon of sin, although Hindu ideas are also largely retained. *The Indian Messenger* gives one of the principles of the Sadharan Brahma Samaj as follows: "To cease from wrong-doing with sincere repentance, is the real expiation." *The Essential Principles of the Brahma Dharma* contain the following:

" Every sinner must suffer the consequences of his own sins sooner or later, in this world or in the next; for the moral law is unchangeable and God's justice irreversible." p. 7.

Brahmos virtually adopt the Buddhist doctrine of *Karma,* which "has no idea of mediation, of satisfaction, of propitiation. Neither in heaven nor in earth can man escape from the consequences of his acts; hence forgiveness and atonement are ideas utterly unknown."

This Brahmist dogma is put in a *quasi*-logical form; but it consists of groundless assertions. Instead of being a " self-evident intuitive truth," it contradicts the testimony of religious conscious-ness. Men instinctively believe in the forgivableness of sin, and instinctively pray for pardon.

Why is an ignorant erring mortal to limit the power of the Almighty? Has he such a thorough knowledge of the Divine administration of the universe to warrant him in proclaiming the unforgivableness of sin? To suppose this is to describe God as weaker than man. An earthly king can pardon an offender, why should this prerogative be denied to the King of kings?

Brahmists hold the doctrine of the Fatherhood of God. An earthly father can forgive the offences of his children; why may not our loving Father in heaven do the same? The Brahmist dogma is opposed to our deepest and tenderest feelings.

The way in which Christianity teaches that sin may be forgiven will now be explained; but before doing so, it is necessary to con-sider the subject of Incarnations.

INCARNATIONS.

In all ages the hope has been more or less entertained that God would become man to lighten the burden of pain and misery under which the world is groaning. Among Hindus the most celebrated incarnations are those of Vishnu. They are usually considered ten in number, although the Bhagavad Purana makes them number-less. Conflicting accounts are given of their origin. Brigu is said to have cursed Vishnu, condemning him to repeated incarnations among mortals. On the other hand, Krishna is represented as say-ing in the Bhagavad Gita: "I am born age after age for the protection of the good, for the destruction of evil-doers, and the establishment of piety." The Kalki Avatar is yet to come, when Vishnu, at the end of the Kali Yug, is to appear seated on a white horse, with drawn sword in his hand blazing like a comet, for the final destruction of the wicked, and the restoration of purity.

On the contrary, Bramhos assert that "God himself never becomes man by putting on a human body." This is opposed to the deepest longings of our heart. The Hindu idea, though very imperfect, is nearer the truth.

Krishna's life on earth, as given in the Bhagavata Purana, cannot be said to have been for the "establishment of piety"; it was rather for the encouragement of vice. Very different was the conduct of the Christian Incarnation. He came also—not for the destruction of sinners—but to save them. A short account of Him will now be given.

The first promise of the true Incarnation was made by God Himself about six thousand years ago. God created man holy; but man, yielding to temptation, fell into sin. God, when He condemned man, graciously gave him the promise of a Saviour. The time when the true Incarnation occurred was nearly 1,900 years ago. The country where He was born, called Judea, lies about midway between India and England.

To become the Saviour of men, the true Incarnation must be man as well as God. If He had been born of woman in the ordinary manner, He would have inherited our sinful nature. He was therefore born from the womb of a pure virgin by the power of God. He was to be called *Jesus*, or Saviour, as the Saviour of world. Another name was *Christ*, which means the anointed one, or one set apart to an office.

Jesus Christ lived at a place called Nazareth, supporting Himself and His mother by working as a carpenter till He was 30 years of age. From that time He began to teach, and to show by many wonderful works that He was the Son of God.

He went about from city to city, and from village to village, doing good. He taught in the house and by the wayside, among the mountains and on the seashore. His teaching was so wonderful that it was said of Him, "Never man spake like this man." He spent whole nights in prayer to His Father.

He healed the sick, cleansed the lepers, opened the eyes of the blind, made the deaf hear, the tongue of the dumb sing, and the lame man leap like a hart. In the desert He fed many thousands with a few loaves and fishes. He raised the dead to life; amid the raging of the sea, He said to the winds and waves, "Peace be still," and at once there was a great calm.

Though Jesus lived a life of spotless purity and went about doing good, wicked men hated Him, because He reproved them for their sins. He came down from heaven to this world to die for our salvation: hence, although He had all power, He allowed Himself

E

to be put to the cruel death of the cross. With nails driven through His hands and feet, He hung on it till He died. He was then buried in a tomb; but on the third day He rose out of it alive. Revealing Himself to His disciples, He commanded them to go into all the world, and make known salvation through Him to every human being. Lastly, ascending through the air in the presence of His disciples, He returned to heaven from which He came.

The Objects of Christ's Incarnation.

As already mentioned, the feeling is universal that man is a sinner, and that sin deserves punishment. Hence sacrifices have existed during all ages and among all nations. The idea that pervades sacrifice is *substitution*. The offerer sometimes laid his hand on the head of the victim saying, " I give thee this life instead of mine." He acknowledged his guilt, but hoped that God would accept the sacrifice in his stead.

Sacrifices prevailed largely among the old Aryans. "The most prominent feature of the Vedic religion," says the Rev. K. S. Macdonald, " is its sacrifices. Scarcely a hymn is found in which sacrifice is not alluded to. The very first verse of the very first hymn runs: 'I glorify Agni, the *purohit* of the sacrifice.' Another hymn says, ' Do thou lead us safe through all sins by the way of sacrifice.' The *Tandya Maha Brahmana* of the *Sama Veda* says of sacrifice, ' Whatever sins we have committed, knowing or unknowing, thou art the annulment thereof. Thou art the annulment of sin—of sin.' "

The same *Brahmana* contains the remarkable statement that " Prajápati, the Lord of creatures, offered himself a sacrifice for the benefit of the *devas*."

Sacrifices were appointed by God to show that sorrow for sin is not enough; that, " without shedding of blood there is no remission." But animal sacrifices were only like a shadow of the great sacrifice that was to be offered, and their chief object was to keep it in remembrance. After the death of the Divine Incarnation, they were to cease.

God created man holy. He was bound to obey God's laws; if he broke them, the penalty was death. Adam, the first man, disobeyed God; all his descendants inherit his sinful nature, and have sinned numberless times in thought, word, and deed.

Since man has broken God's holy laws, he must either suffer or some one must suffer in his stead. God wished to save men, but He could not do so, consistently with His justice, without an atonement.

The object was not to render God merciful. The atonement originated in the love of the Father. It was to show that He is a holy God in hating sin, a righteous God in punishing it, and a merciful God at the same time in forgiving it. The following narrative from Greek history has been used as an illustration :

" Zaleucus, lawgiver of the Locrians, had promulgated a law to his subjects, threatening any one who should be guilty of the crime of adultery, with the loss of his eyes. His own son was the first convicted under the law. The kingly and parental character seemed to struggle for predominance : if the prince be pardoned, what becomes of the law ? if he be punished, how great a calamity will the father endure in the affliction of the son ! What is to be done ? The father determines that he will lose one of his eyes, and the son one of his. It was done. Here was punishment and pardon united. Atonement was made to the offended law, as effectually as if the son had been reduced to total blindness. The letter of the law was not complied with, but the spirit of it was exceeded."*

This made such an impression upon the people, that while Zaleucus presided over the Locrians, no person was again found guilty of adultery.

"The case is not adduced as a perfect parallel to the atonement of Christ, but simply as an illustration of its principles, as tending to show that atonement may be as effectually made by substitution, as by the suffering of the real offender."

God, in His great love to men, as it were, proposed that His only begotten Son should become their substitute, and suffer in their stead. The Son gladly consented, saying, " Lo, I come ;" " I delight to do Thy will."

The objection may be raised that it is unjust that the innocent should suffer for the sins of the guilty. To this the following reply is made.

" It would indeed be most unrighteous in any earthly ruler, were he to seize an innocent person, and make him suffer the sentence of the law, while the culprit himself was allowed to escape. Supposing, however, the purposes of law were equally accomplished, by an innocent person *voluntarily* submitting to death on behalf of a large multitude of offenders who must otherwise have died, there would be no departure from justice ; neither would any alarm be caused to the innocent, by the expectation of being themselves compelled to suffer for the guilty. But if, by such voluntary transference of suffering, those offenders were also reclaimed and made good citizens,—and if moreover he who became their substitute, were restored to life, and as the result of his mediation, were raised to higher honour than before, not only justice would be satisfied, but benevolence would rejoice. So with the sacrifice of Christ. He, the righteous, suffered ; that we, the unrighteous, might escape. But

---

* *The Anxious Inquirer.*

the act was voluntary. The suffering of Christ was brief, while his triumph is everlasting."

Jesus is one; we are millions; but His Divine nature gave an infinite value to His sacrifice. A single diamond, like the *koh-i-nur*, is worth more than crores of ordinary pebbles. God can now pardon the sinner who comes to Him, seeking forgiveness on account of his surety.

Another object of Christ's Incarnation was to work out for us a perfect righteousness by keeping the law which we had broken. To enter heaven it is not enough for a man to be without sin. A stone has that quality. Righteousness is also required. A beggar in filthy rags cannot appear at the durbar of a great King. Our best actions are like them, and clothed in them we cannot appear before God in heaven. Jesus on earth perfectly obeyed God's holy law and His righteousness He gives as a " garment of salvation" to those who accept Him as their Saviour.

A third object of Christ's incarnation was to teach us, and set before us a holy example. His wonderful instructions will be found in the New Testament, and the best way of carrying them out is to seek to follow His steps, to copy His conduct.

Lastly, the exhibition of such love of the Father in giving up His Son, and that of the Son in coming to this world and dying on the cross, was intended to melt the heart of sinners, and made them return to God as repentant prodigals, to make them love Him who so much loved them.

The Christian Method of Obtaining Pardon of Sin.

The great difference between Christianity and all other religions is, that the former teaches *salvation by grace*; the latter *salvation by works*.

Grace here means the *undeserved favour of God*. Some Hindus talk of salvation by grace; but it has already been shown that, by their creed, this is impossible. *Karma* is said to be unalterable even by Brahma. There is no such thing in Hinduism as God's showing favour to any one without his meriting it, and though God is called *dayalu*, or merciful, this is but an empty sound. A criminal after he has undergone the punishment prescribed by law is set free; but this is not called an act of *mercy*. According to Hinduism, *jnana* alone is the cause of salvation, and the effects of works cannot be effaced even by *jnana*. *Jnana* is not a gift from God, but what a man works out for himself.

It is the same with Bramhos. Every sinner must be punished adequately according to his sins, after which he is rewarded according to his merits.

Muhammadans, in like manner, trust for salvation to almsgiving, prayers, pilgrimages, &c.

In all these ways man tries to be his own Saviour, to get to heaven, either on account of his supposed good works or his *jnana.*

The Christian does not look for pardon of sin to anything he can do himself; he looks for salvation through another. There is nothing in this world that exactly corresponds to it; but the following illustration may give some idea of the manner in which pardon is obtained.

A man foolishly got into debt to the amount of a lakh of rupees, and was brought before the king for trial. The debt was proved, the man had nothing to pay, and he must therefore go to prison.

The king's son, hearing of the case, took pity on the culprit, offered to become his security, and to pay his debt.

The king, turning to the criminal, said, "Admit that you deserve punishment. Repent of your misdeeds, Trust my son, and henceforth do as he bids you. His offer will then be accepted, and you will be set free."

To this the debtor replied, "O king, I acknowledge my fault. I accept your son's offer with all my heart. Regarding him henceforth as my redeemer, I will ever trust in him and obey all his commands." Hearing this, the king set the debtor free, and he would have no further cause of fear.

Suppose however, the debtor should say, "Oh king, I reject the offer of your son, and with it your advice that I should henceforth obey him." Would not the king justly order the full penalty of the law to be inflicted upon him?

Sin is compared to debt. Every day we have been adding to it, and so there is, as it were, a long dark catalogue in God's book against us. Although a debtor should pay hereafter for all he gets, this would not wipe away what stood against him. But we cannot even do this. The best men on earth are daily adding to their liabilities.

The punishment of sin is not an earthly prison—but hell. Jesus Christ, the Son of God, wished to save sinners, and offered to assume the debt of all who sought His help. To pay it, He came down from heaven and died on the cross. He offers to become surety for all who accept Him as their Saviour, He answers for their debts, and they are set free. It is but reasonable to expect that they will ever afterward love and obey him.

Those who reject the offer of Jesus Christ and wish to pay their debts themselves, must take the consequences. Their case is far more serious than that of those who never heard of a Saviour, and who will be judged differently.

The Christian looks for salvation to Christ alone—not to any of his own supposed good deeds. His language is, "Lord, save me, I perish." His feeling is expressed in the words :—

> Just as I am,—without one plea,
> But that Thy blood was shed for me,
> And that Thou bid'st me come to Thee,—
>   O Lamb of God, I come !

> Just as I am,—and waiting not,
> To rid my soul of one dark blot,
> To Thee, whose blood can cleanse each spot,
>   O Lamb of God, I come !

Salvation in this manner is fitted to promote two feelings of the utmost importance—*humility* and *love*.

It is very humbling to man's pride to receive salvation as a free gift. He would fain merit it in some degree by his own good works, or at least render himself more worthy of the boon. Pride is entirely excluded by salvation through Christ, and humility is fostered. Love is another feeling awakened. If a person whom we disliked saved our life at the risk of his own, would not ill-feeling be removed, and gratitude kindled? Thus it is with the believer in Christ. There will be love to the Saviour, sorrow for past offences, and an earnest desire to avoid in future every thing displeasing to Him.

Some may object that free salvation through Christ will tempt men to sin : they consider punishments and rewards necessary to secure obedience. But true love is the strongest of all motives. A mother watches over her child with far greater care than a slave who fears the lash, or a hireling who looks to his pay.

The believer, however, is not left to himself. Jesus Christ uses the illustration : " I am the vine, ye are the branches." The true believer is united to Christ, like a branch ingrafted upon a tree. He shares in His life and becomes animated by His spirit.

The Sufficiency of Christ as a Saviour.

There is a common Indian proverb, " Where there is faith, there is God." This means that a man receives simply according to his faith. This saying is considered sufficient, and saves the trouble of all inquiry as to the real value on the object of faith. Let it be examined.

A man's faith may arise from ignorance as well as from knowledge. If a man believes that jewels are gold while they are only brass, will his faith have any effect? If a man intrust his property to a thief believing him to be an honest man, will his faith save his money? If a man take a cooly to be the king, will he be really such? If a man, wishing to cross a deep and rapid river, goes into a leaky boat saying that faith is the chief thing, will this save him from being drowned?

In like manner, if a man worship an idol believing it to be God, will his faith make it God? If a man believes that bathing in the Ganges will wash away his sins, he believes what is untrue and his sin remains.

In worldly matters men are not such fools as to believe that faith is sufficient. A banker does not say this when asked for the loan of money, nor a father when the marriage of his daughter is proposed. Faith placed on a false object is worthless, and simply ruins the man who trusts to it. Our first inquiry should therefore be, Is our faith placed on a proper object?

Hindus may be divided into two great classes,—those belonging to the Vishnu *bhakti* and the Siva *bhakti*. Where did the Hindus learn about them? From the Puranas and other Sastras. It has already been shown that it is a great sin to suppose that God would have acted in the manner in which Vishnu and Siva are said to have done, that he would have been guilty of lying, theft, adultery, and murder.

The Puranas are also full of false geography and astronomy. They assert that there is a Mount Meru in the middle of the earth, 672,000 miles in height, on which there are trees 8,800 miles high, with fruit as large as elephants. There are said to be 1000 islands formed by the 60,000 sons of King Sagar, born in a pumpkin, when they were digging down in search of the horse! Eclipses of the sun and moon are said to be caused by the severed head of the Asura Rahu seeking to seize them.

No intelligent man believes such stories. What the same books contain about Vishnu and Siva is equally fabulous. There are no such beings, and faith in them is vain.

A Saviour must have both the power and the will to help.

Jesus Christ is "mighty to save." It was necessary that He should become man, for it was man who had sinned. Jesus Christ often called Himself the "Son of Man." But He is also the Son of God. This does not mean that He is a Son born in the ordinary way. The supposition were blasphemy. The language is figurative, and only that part of the figure is used which is suitable to the occasion. The human relation of sonship is the nearest explanation that can be given to us. God the Father and the Son are the same in nature, and knit together by the tenderest love.

The Gospel of John begins by referring to the pre-existence of Christ. "In the beginning was the Word, and the Word was with God, and the Word was God." A *word* is that by which we communicate our thoughts. The Son of God may be called "the Word," because by Him God makes known His will to men. John here declares His divinity: "The Word was God." He afterwards mentions His incarnation. "The Word was made flesh and dwelt among us, (and we beheld His glory, the glory as of the only-begotten of the Father) full of grace and truth."

Jesus Christ showed His divinity by His wonderful works already described. It may be said that in the Sastras far more wonderful miracles are related; as Hanuman putting the sun under his arm-pit, and Krishna poising the mountain Govardhana for seven days on his little finger. The difference is that the last are fictions, like Mount Meru.

Jesus Christ, as God, is omnipotent to save all who come to Him.

His *willingness* to save is equally apparent. For this purpose He left the glories of heaven, to dwell as a poor working man upon earth, without a home of His own, exposed to calumny, reproach, and persecution, while fully aware of the painful death upon the cross which was awaiting Him. See how kindly He received all who came to Him! It is frequently said of the sick who sought His help, " He healed them all." When the disciples wished to send away mothers who brought their children to Him, He said, " Suffer the little children to come unto Me and forbid them not."

MEDIATION.

Mediation comes from a word meaning *middle*, or between two. A mediator is a friend of both. He may act merely in a case of ordinary business; but often it is his duty to try to make peace between parties who are at variance with each other. Mediation is one of the peculiar doctrines of Christianity. There are traces of it in Vedic Hinduism. In the Rig-Veda Agni is praised as the messenger of the gods the mediator between gods and men. The doctrine, however, is generally opposed by educated Hindus. " Immediacy" is considered one of the " distinguishing features of Brahmoism." The need of any mediator between God and man is denied; the sinner may at once go into God's presence alone. All this arises from inadequate ideas of the holiness of God and the sinfulness of man.

It is not surprising that Brahmos should have only faint ideas of God's holiness. The gods of their forefathers, as already mentioned, committed sin *in sport*. The greatest of them are charged with the foulest crimes. Brahmos have imbibed some more correct views of God's holiness from Christianity; but still they are very imperfect. In the Bible, the pure spirits before God's throne are represented as crying, " Holy, holy, holy, is the Lord of Hosts." Sin is the greatest abomination in His sight.

Brahmos have also inadequate views of their own sinfulness. This, indeed, is the case with all men. Many think that if they avoid the crimes which would be punishable in a court of justice or bring down upon them condemnation from their associates, they are free from blame. Some comfort themselves with the

thought that they have never done harm to any one. The same
may be said of a sheep or a stone. Men with just views know that
God's "law is exceeding broad," requiring perfect holiness in
thought, word, and deed. Their feeling is expressed in the words,
" We are all as an unclean thing, and all our righteousnesses are as
filthy rags." Truly good men feel that their best actions are defiled
by sin ; that they cannot approach God except through a Mediator.

In ordinary life mediation is of constant occurrence. When a
post is vacant, application is often made through another. An
uncle mediates for his nephew, a teacher interests himself on
behalf of a favourite pupil ; an office is conferred on the son of an
honoured father for the father's sake. Mediation is frequently
employed in case of variance. Two persons have become on ill
terms with each other. It is an excellent plan in such circumstances for one who is a friend of both to mediate. A son who has
behaved very badly and left his father's house, may ask a friend
of his father's to mediate.

If the principle of mediation is well understood and its practice
universally carried out in the affairs of life, why should it be
thought unreasonable to act in the same way in spiritual matters ?
It is far more necessary in the latter than in the former.

God is our Creator, our rightful Lord. We live on His earth ;
everything we have comes from Him. Without His help we could
not live a single moment. Instead of loving and obeying Him, we
have broken His laws and rebelled against His authority. It is
very fitting that in such a case there should be a Mediator, and this
Christianity teaches. The Bible says, "There is one God, and one
Mediator between God and man, the man Christ Jesus."

The Lord Jesus Christ has every qualification necessary on the
part of a mediator. One sinner cannot intercede for another ;
Jesus Christ is sinless. A mediator should be able to enter into
the feelings of both parties. Jesus Christ possesses this quality in
perfection, for He is God as well as man. He knows how God
regards sin and the transgression of His law, and what He requires
for its forgiveness. Jesus Christ, as man, is touched with a feeling
of our infirmities, having been in all points tempted like as we are,
yet without sin.

> Though now ascended up on high
> He bends on earth a brother's eye ;
> Partaker of the human name,
> He knows the frailty of our frame.
>
> In every pang that rends the heart
> The Man of sorrows had a part ;
> He sympathises with our grief,
> And to the sufferer sends relief.

When a debt has been paid, a receipt is given, and the debtor is
set free. The Lord Jesus Christ took upon Himself our sins, and

F

bore the punishment. Pardon is freely offered to all who accept
Him as their Saviour, and ask it in His name. Such confess that
they have no merit in themselves, and seek forgiveness only
through a Mediator.

God, the Father, has appointed Jesus Christ to be the mediator
between Himself and man. Persons who have never heard of
Jesus Christ cannot offer their petitions in His name, and God will
deal justly with them. It is different, however, with others who
know about Jesus Christ, but pass Him over, and offer their requests
in their own name. This shows pride on their part, and is an
insult to God.

A favour is often granted more on account of him who asks it
than for the worthiness of the person on behalf of whom it is made.
Thus if a man like the Duke of Wellington, who had rendered great
service to his country, had asked some favour from the Queen, it
would no doubt have been granted. So it is with the Lord Jesus
Christ. Asking in His name, we are sure to be heard.

The doctrine of mediation is most comforting to a Christian, and
he accepts it with thankfulness. On the other hand, the Hindu
rejects it, and goes into God's presence alone, all defiled with sin.

THE INTERCESSION OF CHRIST.

The work of the Lord Jesus Christ for the salvation of His people
did not end with His ascension to heaven. The Bible says of Him,
" He is able to save them to the uttermost that come unto God by
Him, seeing He ever liveth to make intercession for them." *Intercession* means *going between,* pleading for another. If a king's son
undertook to present a petition to his father, it would probably be
granted ; so it is with the prayers of Christ's people presented by
Himself. We may have kind friends in this world willing to help
us, but they cannot do it long ; they must soon die and leave us.
On the other hand, Jesus lives for ever. Friends may change and
no longer care for us ; Jesus is the same friend for ever. Friends
may be unable though willing to help us ; Jesus has all power,
and is able to save to the uttermost. In the 17th Chapter of the
Gospel of John in the New Testament, we see how Jesus prays for
His people that they may be kept from the evil that is in the world,
that they may love one another, that they may be purified from
sin, and share in His glory.

Christians end their prayers with the words, " for Christ's sake,"
because they ask everything in His name.

FAITH AND REPENTANCE.

The Hindi word for faith is *vishwas.* The word *bhakti* includes
something of what Christians mean by faith, but it means rather
devotion to some particular god.

The error of the common Hindu idea that " Where there is faith, there is God," has been pointed out. Faith in an idol or in a being that has no existence, is worthless. On the other hand, the Lord Jesus " Christ is the mighty God."

The Bible says, "Believe in the Lord Jesus Christ, and thou shalt be saved." Faith is the clinging of the soul to Christ for salvation. We are, as it were, sinking in the deep waters of sin, and in danger of perishing. Jesus Christ throws a rope to us. If we lay hold of it, we are saved by Him. Faith is the act of union to Christ.

Where there is true faith there will be *repentance*. The word in the Bible for repentance means a *change of mind*. It includes sorrow for sin, but chiefly a turning from it.

> Repentance is to leave
> The sins we loved before
> And show that we in earnest grieve
> By doing so no more.

True repentance denotes a turning away from sin as in itself an evil, as hateful to God, and not merely from the fear of punishment.

Faith and repentance are represented in the Bible as the gift of God, but they are to be obtained if sought in the proper way.

While Jesus Christ was on earth, a man, in deep distress, said to Him, "Lord, I believe; help Thou mine unbelief." Though the reader may only be able to

> " Stretch the lame hands of faith and grope,"

let him go to Jesus, saying,

> " Just as I am,—though toss'd about,
> With many a conflict, many a doubt,
> Fightings and fears within, without,
> O Lamb of God, I come !"

ADOPTION.

Adoption denotes the taking as one's own what is another's. It is very common among Hindus to adopt children, who are treated as belonging to the family.

Man, it is true, is a child of God, by creation ; but he has been a rebellious prodigal, and rather chosen Satan as his father. By faith in Jesus Christ, the relation to God is restored, and becomes dearer than ever. When the sinner, as it were, stands before God's bar, he is not only pardoned, but the Judge takes him to His heart, owning him as a child beloved. Well may astonishment be expressed at such an act ! " Behold ! what manner of love the Father hath bestowed upon us, that we should be called the sons of God." This is unknown to Hinduism.

God's adopted sons are to dwell with Him for ever in His heavenly palace. As nothing unholy can enter there, they must first be cleansed from sin. The Agent who does this will next be noticed.

THE HOLY SPIRIT, THE PURIFIER.

Christ was to be called Jesus, the Saviour, because He saves His people from their sins. This is done through the Holy Spirit. It is He who convinces the sinner of his guilt, who inclines him to accept salvation, who gradually uproots what is evil, and implants every holy affection. This doctrine also is peculiar to Christianity. Hinduism has no sanctifier. Brahma, Vishnu, and Siva are represented as stained with foul crimes. How can they, themselves impure, purify their worshippers?

To explain more clearly who the Holy Spirit is, the Christian Trinity will be briefly noticed.

THE TRINITY.

Hinduism has its triads, or threes united. In the Vedas, Agni, Vayu, and Surya, are sometimes associated. A later triad, or *Trimurti*, "triple form," consists of Brahma, Vishnu, and Siva, denoting the creative, preservative, and destructive principles. The Trimurti is represented as one body with three heads. The Christian doctrine, however, is altogether different from this.

Muhammad supposed that the Trinity adored by Christians was God, Jesus Christ, and the Virgin Mary. It is not surprising that the doctrine is strongly opposed by Muhammadans and others by whom it is misunderstood. Rightly known, it is seen to be most honouring to God and comforting to man.

Our own existence is a mystery. We cannot tell how the mind acts upon the body. It is reasonable to suppose that the nature of God is far more mysterious.

Hiero, king of Sicily, said to Simonides a celebrated Greek poet, "what is God?" The philosopher asked a day to consider it. When the king required his answer the next day, Simonides begged two days more. As he kept constantly desiring double the number which he had required before instead of giving his answer; the king asked his reason; "Because," replied the sage, "the longer I meditate on it, the more obscure it appears to me."

The Bible, especially in the Old Testament, declares the absolute unity of God. "The Lord our God is one Lord." "The Lord is God, and there is none else." The same doctrine is taught in the New Testament, as "God is one;" but as has been shown, divinity is also ascribed to Jesus Christ, the Son of God. The same remark applies to the Holy Spirit. The lying of Ananias to the Holy Ghost is described also as lying unto God. Acts, v. 34.

Before Jesus Christ left His disciples, He said to them, "Go ye into all the world, and preach the Gospel to every creature, baptizing them in the name of the Father, Son, and Holy Ghost." This implies that the Divine nature, from which men were to draw their spiritual life and nourishment, is threefold. Accordingly Christians, from the beginning, have ascribed divine honours and a divine name equally to Father, Son, and Holy Ghost. This union of three in one is called the Trinity (*trinus*, threefold), though the term itself does not occur in the Bible.

There may seem to be a contradiction in saying that God is one and yet three. It may be asked, how can one be three and three one? This objection might be valid if the terms were understood in the same sense in each case. But an illustration will show that a living being may be one in one sense and three in another. Man is a unit, yet he consists of body, soul, and spirit. While the comparison is by no means parallel, and can, in no degree, assist us in comprehending the Trinity, it shows that it does not involve any contradiction.

Nothing, merely human, can explain the nature of the Divine Being. When we are told that there are a Father, a Son, and a Holy Spirit, who, from all eternity, have been together, and have exercised special functions in the creation, preservation, and salvation of the universe, we are only to think that the truth has been presented to us in such a form as can best be understood. All that we can expect to know is what is needful for us at present. We still only "see through a glass darkly," and this applies specially to the Divine nature.

But the doctrine, rightly understood, is fitted to awaken in us feelings of the warmest adoration and praise. Father, Son, and Holy Spirit have gloriously united for man's redemption. The Father so loved the world that He gave up His only Son; the Son so loved us as to die for us; the Holy Spirit bears with our innumerable provocations and seeks to purify us. Well may it be said, "Who is a God like unto Thee?" "O the depth of the riches both of the wisdom and knowledge of God!"

MEANS OF PURIFICATION.

Hindus rely mainly upon bathing in the Ganges or other waters as a means of purifying from sin. The worthlessness of this is apparent. How many shopkeepers, living on the banks of the Ganges, go daily from its waters to their shops to lie and cheat their customers in every possible way. The Mahratta Brahmans, living far away from the Ganges, claim the superior sanctity of the Narbada. "One day's ablution in the Ganges," say they, "frees from all sin; but the mere sight of the Narbada purifies from guilt." Pilgrimages, smearing with sacred ashes, swallowing the five products of the cow, &c., are equally vain.

The means prescribed by Christianity are very different. These will now be explained, but it is to be remembered that it is the Holy Spirit who gives them efficacy. It is He who is ever present with His people, guiding them, and bringing them at last without spot or blemish to the purity and blessedness of heaven.

1. *The Daily Study of the Scriptures.*

Hindus believe that the mere reading, or even hearing of their Sastras, whether understood or not, is meritorious. The Vishnu Purana says, "Hearing this Purana but once is as efficacious as the offering of oblations in a perpetual fire for a year." Reading stories of unholy gods cannot purify those who hear them—rather the reverse according to the proverb, *yatha devah tatha bhaktah,* As is the god so is the worshipper.

Christianity teaches that the Bible is the great book given by God for man's guidance and growth in holiness. In the last prayer of Jesus Christ for His disciples before His death, He said, " Sanctify them through Thy truth ; Thy word is truth." The benefit received will, however, depend upon the manner in which the duty is performed. A chapter may be hurriedly gone over without thought or profit.

The Bible should be read with prayer. Say, " O God, open Thou mine eyes that I may behold wondrous things out of Thy law. Open, Lord, my understanding that I may understand the Scriptures. Write Thy laws upon my heart."

The object should be, not to get over so many verses, but to dwell upon the meaning and bearing of what is read. A little, well thought out, is better than a great deal gone over carelessly. We should meditate on what we read till the truth which is in it becomes our own, and promotes our spiritual growth. We should apply what we read to the regulation of our lives. The Bible thus studied will prove a light to the feet, and a lamp to the path.

It is a good plan to have a text of Scripture to be specially remembered each day. There are little books containing a text of Scripture and a verse of a hymn for every day in the year, as " Daily Food." Such may be used with advantage; but they should not be allowed to supersede the study of the Bible itself.

2. *Private Prayer.*

The prayers of the Hindus are chiefly for temporal blessings. The petitions in the Rig Veda are for rain, cattle, horses, male children, the destruction of enemies, &c. A great French Sanskrit

scholar sums them in the words, " Here is butter ; give us cows."
There are only a very few hymns to Varuna in which pardon of sin
is sought; and even these generally end with a request for wealth.

Varuna is no longer worshipped, and prayers for holiness cannot
be offered to Vishnu or Siva.

The prayers of Hindus often consist merely in the repetition of
the names of their gods. If a son kept crying, " Father, father,
father," and said nothing more, he would be thought to be mad.
The father would say, " tell me what you want." Jesus Christ
condemns such vain repetitions.

While Christianity sanctions prayer for temporal blessings, its
main petitions are for the pardon of sin, holiness, and the spread of
God's kingdom. The disciples of Jesus Christ when he was on
earth, said to him, " Lord, teach us to pray." His reply was :—
After this manner pray ye :

" Our Father which art in heaven, Hallowed be Thy name, Thy
kingdom come. Thy will be done on earth as it is in heaven. Give
us this day our daily bread. And forgive us our debts as we forgive our debtors. And lead us not into temptation, but deliver us
from evil. For Thine is the kingdom, and the power, and the glory,
for ever, Amen."

Prayer has been called the " breath of the Christian." A man can
no more be a true Christian without prayer than he can live without breathing. There should be at least morning and evening prayer ; but often throughout the day the heart should be lifted up to
God. Any temptation specially calls for Divine help.

Of all petitions, the most earnest should be for the gift of the Holy
Spirit. Every other blessing follows in its train. The following
words may express the feeling which should be cherished :

> More of Thy presence, Lord, impart ;
> More of Thine image let me bear ;
> Erect Thy throne within my heart,
> And reign without a rival there.

Prayer is the desire of the heart. It is best expressed in our
own words, and in the language with which we are most familiar.

Some examples of prayer, both for religious inquirers and Christians, are given in " Prayers for Students and Others."*

3. *Public Worship.*

Hindu and Christian public worship are very different from each
other. In Vedic times Hindu worship consisted of offerings and
sacrifices. The products of the cow were offered—milk, curds, and
butter. Grain was offered, fried, boiled, or as flour balls. Sacrifices
included goats, sheep, cows, buffaloes, horses, men—the last two

---

* Price ½ Anna. With Postage 1 Anna. May be obtained from Mr. A. T. Scott
Tract Depôt, Madras.

being considered of the greatest value. The intoxicating Soma
juice was the most common offering. Indra was invited to drink it
like a thirsty stag.

Modern Hindus, who now worship the cow, can scarcely believe
that their Aryan forefathers sacrificed her and ate her flesh.
But times without number, the Vedas refer to ceremonies called
Gomedha, in which the cow was sacrificed. A thick-legged cow
was sacrificed to Indra, a barren cow to Vishnu, a red cow to
Rudra, &c.

Modern Hindu worship will next be described. One of the
most celebrated temples in India is that of Bhuvanesvara in
Orissa. Siva is there worshipped under the form of a large un-
carved block of granite, about 8 feet long, partly buried in the
ground, partly apparent above the soil to the height of about 8 inches.
The block is believed to be a linga of the Svayambhu class, pervaded of their own nature by the essence of the deity.

Dr. Rajendralala Mitra thus describes the daily worship, consisting of no less than 22 ceremonial acts :—

" (1) At the first appearance of dawn, bells are rung to rouse the deity
from his slumbers ; (2) a lamp with many wicks is waved in front of the
stone ; (3) the god's teeth are cleaned by pouring water and rubbing a
stick about a foot long on the stone ; (4) the deity is washed and bathed
by emptying several pitchers of water on the stone ; (5) the god is dressed
by putting clothes on the stone; (6) the first breakfast is offered, consisting
of grain, sweetmeats, curd, and cocoanuts ; (7) the god has his principal
breakfast, when cakes and more substantial viands are served ; (8) a kind
of little lunch is offered ; (9) the god has his regular lunch ; (10) the
mid-day dinner is served, consisting of curry, rice, pastry, cakes, cream, &c.,
while a priest waves a many-flamed lamp and burns incense before the
stone ; (11) strains of noisy discordant music rouse the deity from his
afternoon sleep at 4 P. M., the sanctuary having been closed for the pre-
ceding four hours ; (12) sweetmeats are offered ; (13) the afternoon bath
is administered ; (14) the god is dressed as in the morning ; (15) another
meal is served ; (16) another bath is administered ; (17) the full dress
ceremony takes place, when fine costly vestments, yellow flowers, and
perfumery are placed on the stone ; (18) another offering of food follows ;
(19) after an hour's interval the regular supper is served ; (20) five masks
and a Damaru, used in dancing, are brought in and oblations made to them ;
(21) waving of lights before bedtime ; (22) a bedstead is brought into the
sanctuary and the god composed to sleep.

Lastly, the god is sometimes told, " Parvati awaits you."

The worship of Vishnu is much of the same character, but no
animal food is offered.

Bishop Caldwell says : " The duties of life are never inculcated
in any Hindu temple. The discharge of those duties is never
represented as enjoined by the gods, nor are any prayers ever
offered in any temple for help to enable the worshippers to discharge those duties aright."

While there is nothing in Hindu public worship fitted to purify, in some cases there is much having a contrary influence. Connected with many of the temples in South India, there are dancing girls, called *devadasi*, handmaidens of the gods. Thus avowed prostitutes take a prominent part in Hindu religious worship. According to the Madras Census of 1881, the number of "female dancers" in the Presidency was 11,573. It was the same with Greek worship in ancient times. The indignant words of Bishop Lightfoot may be applied to India :—

" Imagine, if you can, this licensed shamelessness, this consecrated profligacy, carried on under the sanction of religion and in the full blaze of publicity, while statesmen and patriots, philosophers and men of letters, looked on unconcerned, not uttering one word and not raising one finger to put it down."

Public worship among Christians consists in united prayer, the reading of the Bible, singing hymns, and a sermon or address. The form varies somewhat. To give a better idea of it, a short account will be given of the religious service at which the Queen Empress of India is present every Sunday. First a verse of the Bible, like the following, is read :

" I will arise and go to my father, and will say unto him, Father, I have sinned against heaven, and before thee, and am no more worthy to be called thy son."

The people are then invited to confess their sins in the following words :—

" Almighty and most merciful Father, we have erred and strayed from Thy ways like lost sheep. We have followed too much the devices and desires of our own hearts. We have offended against Thy holy laws. We have left undone those things which we ought to have done ; and we have done those things which we ought not to have done ; and there is no health in us. But Thou, O Lord, have mercy upon us, miserable offenders. Spare Thou them, O God, which confess their faults. Restore Thou them that are penitent; according to Thy promises declared unto mankind in Christ Jesu our Lord. And grant, O most merciful Father, for His sake, that we may hereafter live a godly, righteous, and sober life, to the glory of Thy holy Name. *Amen.*"

Passages are read from the Bible, teaching the people what they are to believe and do. The Minister stands up, and, in the name of God, enjoins the worshippers not to steal, not to bear false witness, not to commit adultery, not to commit any of the four offences against God or of the six offences against man forbidden in the Ten Commandments, and then after each proclamation of a commandment, he joins with the people in asking God to have mercy upon them, and to give them grace to keep that commandment better in future. There is no such teaching of morality as this by any Brahman or priest in any temple in all India.

G

The singing of hymns is an important part of Christian worship. The following is a translation of one which has been used for nearly 3000 years :

> Before Jehovah's awful throne,
>   Ye nations, bow with sacred joy ;
> Know that the Lord is God alone ;
>   He can create, and He destroy.
>
> His sovereign power, without our aid,
>   Made us of clay, and formed us men ;
> And when like wandering sheep we strayed,
>   He brought us to His fold again.
>
> We are His people, we His care,—
>   Our souls and all our mortal frame :
> What lasting honours shall we rear,
>   Almighty Maker, to Thy name ?
>
> We'll crowd Thy gates with thankful songs,
>   High as the heavens our voices raise ;
> And earth, with her ten thousand tongues,
>   Shall fill Thy courts with sounding praise.
>
> Wide as the world is Thy command,
>   Vast as eternity Thy love ;
> Firm as a rock Thy truth must stand
>   When rolling years shall cease to move.

The following thanksgiving is used towards the close of the prayers :—

" Almighty God, Father of all mercies, we Thine unworthy servants do give Thee most humble and hearty thanks for all Thy goodness and loving-kindness to us and to all men. We bless Thee for our creation, preservation, and all the blessings of this life ; but above all, for Thine inestimable love in the redemption of the world by our Lord Jesus Christ ; for the means of grace, and for the hope of glory. And, we beseech Thee, give us that due sense of all Thy mercies, that our hearts may be un- feignedly thankful, and that we show forth Thy praise, not only with our lips, but in our lives ; by giving up ourselves to Thy service, and by walking before Thee in holiness and righteousness all our days ; through Jesus Christ our Lord, to whom with Thee and the Holy Ghost be all honour and glory, world without end. *Amen.*"

Then follows a sermon, an address explaining some doctrine or enforcing some duty.

Let any intelligent honest Hindu contrast Christian public wor- ship with that of Hindu temples, and say which is preferable. The Bramhos have adopted much the same form ; but it was borrowed from Christianity.

Besides public worship, Christians join in the observance of what is called the Lord's Supper, in memory of Christ's death, showing their unity with each other and with Him and as a means of spiri- tual nourishment.

4. *The due observance of Sunday or the Lord's Day.*

Hindus have numerous festivals throughout the year; but they have no special day of the week for worship. When man was created, the seventh day of the week was appointed to be observed as a day of rest. It was called *Sabbath*, from a Hebrew word meaning *rest*. Jesus Christ rose from the dead on the first day of the week, which is now observed by Christians instead of the seventh day. It is sometimes called Sunday from the name of the day of the week ; but the Lord's Day, or the Christian Sabbath, is more appropriate.

The appointment of a day of rest is a great blessing to man. It gives the busy labourer a day at home with his own family. The change of thought is refreshing to the mind. The influence of the Christian Sabbath is very considerable in promoting the happiness and civilization of a community. But it is of chief advantage as an opportunity of moral and religious culture. It calls the thoughts away from merely secular employments, and invites us to the contemplation of those higher truths which concern our eternal well-being.

On the Lord's Day, ordinary duties should be laid aside, and we should devote more time than on other days to the reading of the Scriptures and religious books. Meditation is another duty. There should be a careful review of our moral and religious conduct during the past week, and any circumstances calling for special watchfulness during the coming week, should be considered. Earnest prayer for pardon and strength to resist temptation, should accompany the exercise.

The public worship of God, already mentioned, is one of the chief duties of the Lord's Day. It has a most beneficial influence in several respects.

5. *The Reading of suitable Christian Books.*

While the Bible should be the chief study, some other books may be read with advantage. A good *Hymn Book* should perhaps rank next to the Bible. Numerous books have been provided for English Christians. Doddridge's *Rise and Progress of Religion in the Soul* is valued by earnest inquirers. Pike's *Guide for Young Disciples* is a useful work, more recent. *The Pilgrim's Progress* is a favourite all the world over.

6. *Intercourse with Christian Friends.*

Provided they are of the right stamp, few means are more profitable. " Iron sharpeneth iron ; so a man sharpeneth the countenance of his friend." Prayer, the study of the Scriptures, and conversation on the Christian life, should occupy such little gather-

7. *Self-Examination and Meditation.*

Most men live at random.   Their actions are guided by the im-
pulse of the moment.   Before doing any thing, the question should
always be asked, Is this right ?   The man who does not use his
reason is scorned as a fool.   It is still more inexcusable to act
without consulting conscience beforehand.   There should also be
careful consideration afterwards.   The rule of old Pythagoreans
is thus given :—

> " Let not soft sleep usurp oblivious sway
>   Till thrice you've told the deeds that mark'd the day ;
>   Whither thy steps ? what good for thee most fitted
>   Was aptly done ? and what good deed omitted ?
>   And when you've summed the tale, wipe out the bad
>   With gracious grief, and in the good be glad !"

" No man," says Blackie, " will ever attain to high excellence in
what an excellent old divine calls ' The life of God in the soul of
man,' without cultivating stated periods of solitude, and using that
solitude for the important purpose of self-knowledge and self-
amelioration.   ' Commune with your own heart on your bed and be
still,' said the Psalmist."

But this is not enough.   The prayer of the Psalmist should also
be ours : " Search me, O God, and know my heart ; try me, and
know my thoughts ; and see if there be any wicked way in me, and
lead me in the way everlasting."

8. *Watchfulness against Temptation.*

The Lord Jesus Christ, shortly before His death, gave this caution
to His disciples, " Watch and pray that ye enter not into temptation."   This should never to be forgotten.   In many cases where we
have fallen into sin, experience tells us that we might have avoided
the fall by avoiding the temptation.   This caution is especially
necessary in the case of the young.   Ungodly companions and bad
books are to be carefully shunned.   Some temptations we must
meet, and " blessed is the man that endureth temptation."   The
rule applies to going into *needless* temptation.   When called by duty
to trial, there should be special watchfulness and prayer.

9. *Abiding in Christ.*

Sad experience teaches Christ's followers the truth of His words,
" Without me ye can do nothing." Jesus said to His disciples, " I am
the vine, ye are the branches.   As the branch cannot bear fruit of
itself except it abide in the vine ; no more can ye except ye abide
in me."   True Christians are united to Christ by faith.   Their
language is, " Lord what wouldst Thou have me to do ?" They seek
to be guided by His wisdom, and to be upheld by His strength.

PROFESSION OF RELIGION.

Some Hindus have no outward signs of the religious sect to which they belong; but it is otherwise with many. In South India, where Saivas are most numerous, the forehead, and sometimes the body, is smeared with the ashes of cowdung. A common saying is " The forehead without sacred ashes is void of beauty."

Vaishnavas often wear a mark on the forehead intended to represent the foot of their deity. The marks differ according to the sect. Some are branded on the body.

Mothers sometimes refuse to give food to their children till they have put on these marks.

Christianity has no outward marks; but it has baptism, which is a sign of its profession. Baptism is a washing with water in the name of the Father, the Son, and the Holy Spirit. As water cleanses the body, so the Holy Spirit cleanses the soul from sin. Baptism also denotes admission into the Christian Church, union with Christ, and is a promise on the part of the recipient to continue His faithful soldier until the end of life. In many cases it is a mere form; but when truly observed such is its meaning.

Soldiers have flags denoting the king they serve. Marks on the forehead and baptism may be compared to these flags. They proclaim openly who is worshipped.

The great question is, To whom is allegiance justly due? The greatest crime in a state is rebellion against the rightful sovereign.

Our consciences tell us that the one true God must be holy. Can Siva or Vishnu lay any claim to such a character? It is a vain excuse to say that drunkenness, adultery, and murder were not sins in them. On the contrary, it would be a far greater sin for God to be guilty of such conduct than for us. Hindu marks on the forehead show that the wearer, instead of worshipping the one true God of spotless holiness, his Creator, Preserver, and rightful King, has rebelled against Him and chosen in preference one who is reputed to have been guilty of the crimes above mentioned. No witnesses are necessary. The mark on the forehead convicts the wearer of high treason.

Some may say that although they wear ashes or the Vaishnava sign, they in reality worship the one true God. Suppose that men have risen in rebellion and many have placed themselves under their flag. Would the rightful King be satisfied with the excuse, " True, we are under the flag of your enemies, but secretly we serve you." Such men would be punished equally with others. It is well known what Hindus understand by Siva and Vishnu, and to mean something entirely different is fraud. The God of truth is not to be worshipped by hypocrites.

But there are other marks than ashes or the trident pointing out whom we serve. Abusive language, lying, covetousness; impurity,

&c., are also marks which prove that we are rebels against God. On the other hand, just, meek, loving, pure, and holy conduct shows that we are God's true followers.

PROSPECTS AT DEATH.

The only thing a human being knows with certainty about his future lot is, that he must die. To every one must come that

Inevitable Day,
When a voice to me shall say,
' Thou must rise and come away ;
All thine other journeys past,
Gird thee and make ready fast
For thy longest and thy last.'

What are the prospects of a thoughtful Hindu at death ? According to the doctrine of *Karma*, there is no forgiveness of sin. He has not merely the transgressions of this life to answer for, but those of countless former births. Numbers, it is true, die like brutes heedless of the future or indulging vain hopes on account of their supposed merit ; but a thoughtful Hindu may well "meditate terror." Suppose even that he has good deeds, what are his prospects ?

"The being who is still subject to birth may at one time sport in the beautiful garden of a heavenly world, and at another be cut to a thousand pieces in hell ; at one time he may be one of the highest gods and at another a degraded outcast ; at one time he may feed on ambrosia and at another he may have molten lead poured down his throat. Alternately he may repose on a couch with the gods and writhe on a bed of red hot iron ; become wild with pleasure and then mad with pain ; sit on the throne of the gods and then be impaled with hungry dogs around."

Hindus, it is true, may die full of hope. Professor Wilson, a great Sanskrit scholar, says : " It matters not how atrocious a sinner may be, if he paints his face, his breast, his arms with certain sectarial marks ; or, which is better, if he brands his skin permanently with them with a red hot stamp ; if he is constantly chanting hymns in honour of Vishnu ; or, what is equally efficacious, if he spends hours in the simple reiteration of his name or names ; if he die with the word Hari or Rama or Krishna on his lips, and the thought of him in his mind, he may have lived a monster of iniquity—he is certain of heaven."

Such a man, however, dies with a lie in his right hand ; he is only self-deceived. Instead of being taken up to heaven, he will be dragged down to hell.

It is allowed that the anticipations of a wicked nominal Christian are still worse ; he must die without hope. On the other hand, the true believer in Christ can look forward to the future with joy. He can use words like the following : "Though I walk through the valley of the shadow of death, I will fear no evil." "O Death where is thy sting? O grave, where is thy Victory?" "I am now ready to be offered up and the time of my departure is at hand. I have fought a good fight, I have finished my course, I have kept the faith : henceforth there is laid up for me a crown of righteousness." "We know that if our earthly house of this tabernacle were dissolved, we have a building of God, a house not made with hands eternal in the heaven."

Jesus Christ said to the thief on the cross, "To-day shalt thou be with me in paradise." The very day the true Christian dies, he is happy with Christ.

Which prospect is the more comforting in a dying hour? Reader, what is your hope?

FUTURE STATE.

The great aim of Hinduism is to cut short the 84 lakhs of births, to arrive at *mukti* or absorption. "Just as rivers falling into the sea lose their names and forms, so wise men, losing their names and forms, attain the *Paratpara Purusha*."

As already mentioned, illustration with Hindus passes for argument. Rivers mixing with the sea is no proof that men may be absorbed into the Divine being. Only substances of the same kind mix. But God is different from any other being ; there is none like Him. How, then, can any other be absorbed in Him?

Granting, however, that absorption does take place, what does it amount to? Brahm is said to exist in a state of dreamless sleep, without any more thought than a stone. Hindu absorption is practically the same as the Buddhist *nirvana* or annihilation. "Not to be," says Professor Wilson, "is the melancholy result of the religion and philosophy of the Hindus."

Some Hindus, it is true, look for a future conscious existence with Vishnu or Siva; but there are no such beings. Belief in them is based on the same Puranas which teach the existence of Mount Meru. The one is no more true than the other. What intelligent man can believe in a god supposed to have had wives and children and to have been stained with crime?

Christianity denies the doctrine of transmigration, and teaches that the future state of each man is fixed at death. The wicked are for ever miserable, the righteous are for ever happy.

So long as man sins, he must suffer ; and we have no reason to believe that in a future state a man will repent.

The other state is one of unending joy in the presence of God. It can be described only in the language of earth. It is said of the righteous : "They shall hunger no more, neither thirst any more, and God shall wipe away all tears from their tears." Heaven is compared to a city whose streets are of pure gold, as it were transparent glass. Those who enter it are represented as having crowns on their head, palms in their hands, and golden harps to sing the praises of Him who redeemed them. The great happiness of heaven is that it is *eternal*. There is no passing from heaven to hell as according to Hinduism. Those who enter there shall be "for ever with the Lord." The Christian does not get to heaven by his own merit, but as a gift of God, and hence he has no fear of his merit being exhausted, and that he will have to fall down again to this world of sin and sorrow.

Bunyan, in the *Pilgrim's Progress*, after describing in vision the inhabitants of the heavenly city, adds "Which, when I had seen, I wished myself among them."

Comparative Effects of Hinduism and Christianity.

"By their fruits ye shall know them," is an excellent test. A religion from God, the fountain of goodness, should increase the worldly prosperity of those who embrace it, promote education, give equal rights to all, check vice, encourage virtue, and give ennobling ideas of its author. The effects of a religion are best shown, not by its results on individuals, but by its influence on nations. India and England may be taken as standards in this respect.

For three thousand years Hinduism, in different forms, has been the religion of India. What are the results?

There are great complaints about the poverty of the country. Hinduism has increased it by making manual labour degrading, by hindering foreign commerce, by encouraging idle vagrants, by its indiscriminate charity, its fatalism. The people, like children, squander their money on jewels and idle show, instead of turning it to good account.

Two thousand years ago the inhabitants of the British Islands were little better than barbarians. In the south a little grain was raised; in the middle, the people subsisted chiefly on their flocks and herds; in the north, they were in a savage state, living on wild fruits, by hunting and fishing. England is now one of the richest countries in the world.

The Bible says, "Godliness is profitable unto all things, having promise of the life that now is, and of that which is to come."

Has Hinduism promoted education? The Brahmans jealously sought to confine knowledge to themselves. The Vedas were not written, lest the other castes should read them. Education and religious instruction were denied to Sudras. There is a proverb that the sayings of wisdom in the mouth of a Sudra are as butter in the mouth of a dog. Even at present, only one in five of the people can read.

Two thousand years ago the ancient British were without a written language; now education is universal, and England has produced some of the greatest writers that have ever lived.

When Christian Missionaries came to India, one of the first things they did was to open schools—not for certain castes, but for all—for the most degraded.

Hinduism has taught women to regard their husbands as their gods; it has denied them education and religious instruction; it has fostered early marriages; it has originated the cruel treatment of widows; it encouraged widow-burning. Women have been degraded, and they have dragged the men down to their level.

In England, women are educated and have the same religious privileges as men. It is this which has largely contributed to raise England to the high position she at present occupies.

Has Hinduism given equal rights to all? Its chief feature is caste, which it stamps with Divine authority. It has sought to exalt some as *Bhúdévas*, gods on earth, while it has degraded others beneath the brutes. It has crushed individual liberty, and made the people the victims of the most abject social and religious tyranny. Hindu disunion, by caste, has made the country an easy prey to foreign nations.

The second great Commandment of Christianity is, "Thou shalt love thy neighbour as thyself," that is, we should treat others as we wish them to act towards ourselves. Christianity teaches the Fatherhood of God and the Brotherhood of man, that we are all descended from the same first parents, that we should look upon all men as brethren, and seek to do them good.

Has Hinduism checked vice and encouraged virtue? No instruction in morals is given in its temples, some of which are disgraced by most indecent sculptures; in many cases prostitutes take a prominent part in its religious services; its principal gods are described in its own Sastras as guilty of great crimes.

Christianity teaches that the one true God is of spotless holiness, that sin is "the abominable thing which He hates;" it holds up for our imitation the Lord Jesus Christ who went about doing good; in its public worship, sin of every kind is forbidden, and holiness is inculcated.

It is true that there are a number of wicked people in England, who know nothing of Christianity; and even of those who do know, many prefer to follow their own selfish and evil desires. There is, however, this difference between Englishmen and Hindus; a bad Englishman is acting contrary to his religion; a bad Hindu is only imitating the example of his gods. But, taken as a whole, Christianity has had a great effect in raising the moral character of the people of England.

What ideas has Hinduism given of God? It has taught the people to combine pantheism and polytheism, its deities numbering 33 crores; it has made the land full of idols, and encouraged the

H

worship of brutes, beasts, stocks, and stones. "As is the god, so is
the worshipper." The people, though possessing excellent natural
abilities, have, in some respects, become as unintelligent as the
objects of their worship. Like the lower animals, they are mainly
guided by custom, and are the easy victims of priestcraft, believing
the most extravagant fables, and accepting the most contradictory
statements. Christianity teaches monotheism, and presents the
loftiest conceptions of God in every respect : it strictly forbids all
image worship.

Hinduism is a religion only for Hindus. People must by birth
belong to the four castes. Christianity is a universal religion, wel-
coming the whole human race.

Hinduism calls this the Kali Yug, and expects things to become
worse and worse, till a man becomes grey at 12 years of age. It
has been the enemy of progress, and has led to a stationary state
of semi-civilisation in India.

Christianity looks for a gradual improvement, ending in a reign
of peace and righteousness. As Gladstone says, "For the last
fifteen hundred years Christianity has always marched in the van
of all human improvement and civilization, and it has harnessed to
its car all that is great and glorious in the human race."

It is true that great crimes, such as religious persecution, have
been perpetrated in the name of Christianity ; but they are
abhorrent to its spirit. They are the remains of the old heathen
spirit which made the king of Babylon threaten to throw into
a fiery furnace all who would not worship the golden idol he had
set up.

The desire for reform which now animates some educated Indians
has been derived from Christianity, while the Reactionists are
inspired by Hinduism.

It is cheerfully allowed that in some Hindu books there are, here
and there, sublime descriptions of God ; but they are neutralised
by others of an opposite character. A learned writer on the
Nyaya philosophy begins his book with the adoration of Krishna,
whom he calls, at once, "the seed of the tree of the universe," and
"the stealer of the clothes of the young Gopis."

The Hindus themselves have also some excellent qualities.
Many of them, morally, are much better than their gods ; whereas
the best Christians fall infinitely below the object of their
worship.

Hinduism has either originated or aggravated some of the worst
evils from which India suffers—especially its ignorance, its dreami-
ness, its fatalism, the degradation of its women, its social bondage,
its superstition ; while it has been the chief obstacle to progress in
every respect. The substitution of Christianity would be as life
from the dead.

SUMMARY.

While Hinduism and Christianity agree on some points, such as the need of a revelation and man's sinfulness; there are many most important differences. A summary of the contrasts is given below.

GOD.

The chief Hindu system teaches pantheism, that nothing else exists but God. Its watchword is *ekamevádvitíyam*, one only without a second, or, *Sarvam khalvidam Brahma*, all this is Brahma. Christianity teaches that God and the universe which He has created are distinct.

Hinduism teaches polytheism, the doctrine of many gods, as well as pantheism, its divinities varying from thrice-eleven to 33 crores. Christianity teaches monotheism, or, that there is only one God.

Hinduism represents Brahma in his usual state as *nirguna*, in a dreamless sleep; Christianity teaches that God is never unconscious.

Hinduism represents Brahma in his *saguna* condition as possessing *rajas*, passion, and *tamas*, darkness, as well as *sattva*, truth: Christianity declares God to be light without darkness at all, to be spotlessly holy.

Hinduism has its Trimurti, or triple form: Christianity, the doctrine of the Trinity, the three-one God; but the two doctrines are altogether different.

CREATION AND GOVERNMENT OF THE WORLD.

Christianity teaches that God created all things out of nothing by His powerful word: Hinduism, that God did not create anything, that *prakriti* or *maya* is eternal, and all that Brahma does is to arrange it.

According to Vedantism, all is *maya*, illusion. Christianity affirms the reality of the universe and of our personal existence.

Christianity teaches that God governs the world. Hinduism that every thing is regulated by *Adrishta, Karma,* or fate.

MAN.

Christianity teaches that God created man, that He is our Father in heaven. Hinduism affirms that souls are eternal. Hence our relation to God is not that of Creator and creature, father and child, but of beings co-eternal and mutually independent; or, according to Vedantism, of portions to the whole.

Christianity teaches that we did not exist before our birth in this world: Hinduism, that we have passed already through countless births, and will do the same in future.

Hinduism teaches that all life is the same,—that a man may become in a future birth a beast, a fish, an insect, or a vegetable.

Christianity, that man is and ever remains distinct from every other creature.

Christianity teaches the Brotherhood of man.   Hinduism teaches that God has divided Indians into four castes, while all others are impure Mlechhas or outcastes.

SIN.

Hinduism denies the eternal distinction between right and wrong. " To the mighty is no sin." Christianity affirms it, and declares that it would be far worse for God to sin than for man.

Christianity teaches us to seek to be like God; the Bhagavat Purana warns its readers not to imitate the conduct of Krishna.

Hinduism thinks so lightly of sin that the gods are said sometimes to commit it as a " divine sport:" Christianity declares it to be " that abominable thing which God hates."

Christianity teaches that man is a free agent : Hindnism, that his fate has been written by Brahma on his head, and that it is unalterable.

Christianity teaches the doctrine of personal responsibility : Hinduism, that a man must follow the custom of his caste.

The only sin which a Hindu regards as unpardonable is to break the rules of caste : Christianity teaches that sin is to break the laws of God.

A Hindu may be guilty of lying, theft, oppression, adultery, murder, without losing caste; but let him eat with a European or a man of a different caste, or marry a widow, &c., and he is expelled.   Christianity teaches that a man is defiled, not by what he eats, but by evil thoughts, words, and actions.

SALVATION.

Salvation, according to Hinduism, usually means deliverance from future births and absorption into Brahm ; according to Christianity, it is deliverance from sin, and an eternal conscious existence full of joy in heaven.

Christianity and Hinduism both admit that man is sinful; but they differ widely as to the means of his purification.

Hinduism is self-contradictory with regard to the pardon of sin. According to *karma*, it is impossible to escape the fruit of former deeds ; but the common belief is that the worst sins may be washed away by bathing in the Ganges or even by taking the name of some god.   Christianity teaches that God can pardon sin ; but asserts the worthlessness of all human methods for its removal.

Christianity teaches that man's highest duty is to glorify God and do good to his fellow-creatures : Hinduism, that it is to refrain from all actions, good, bad, or indifferent, and obtain absorption into Brahm.

Christianity and Hinduism have both their incarnations; but Christ and Krishna are as different as light and darkness.

Hinduism teaches that man is to be his own saviour: Christianity, that God alone can save him.

Hinduism teaches that a man is rewarded in heaven according to his *meritorious works :* Christianity teaches salvation by *grace,* without any merit of man's own.

Hinduism teaches that absorption is obtained by *jnana,* when a man can say *Aham Brahmasmi,* I am Brahma: Christianity teaches that such an expression is blasphemous.

Christianity teaches that sinful man needs a mediator: Hinduism and Brahmoism reject the doctrine.

The Hindu proverb is that " Where there is faith there is God :" Christianity teaches that faith must have a proper object.

The *prayaschitta* of Hinduism is to swallow the five products of the cow and give feasts to Brahmans: the repentance required by Christianity is a heart-felt sorrow for sin, and a turning from it.

Christianity teaches that man is purified by God's Holy Spirit; no Hindu god is himself pure, and such being the case, he cannot make others pure.

SCRIPTURES.

Christianity has its Bible for all; Hinduism its Sastras for Brahman men only ; but as they are contradictory, they cannot both be true.

Hinduism teaches that the mere hearing of its Sastras is meritorious ; Christianity requires the Bible to be read with understanding and prayer.

WORSHIP.

Christianity forbids the worship of any other than the one true God : Hinduism allows the worship of any thing in heaven above or in the earth beneath, even brute beasts, reptiles, plants, and stones.

Christianity strictly forbids the worship of God through images : Hinduism has made India a "land full of idols."

Hinduism teaches that the mere repetition of God's name is prayer : Christianity, that prayer is the desire of the heart.

Hinduism attaches the greatest virtue to austerities : Christianity teaches that they are worthless for man's salvation.

Hinduism has no teaching of man's duty in its temples; its worship of images is degrading, and where there are dancing girls, its temple service is corrupting : Christian worship is elevating, being fitted to give a hatred of sin and a desire for holiness.

Christianity has one day in seven set apart for Divine worship and progress in holiness ; Hinduism has its festivals, but they have no good moral influence.

Hinduism has its mark on the forehead or branding of the body : Christianity has baptism, denoting the need of cleansing from sin.

PROSPECTS AT DEATH.

The most devout Hindu cannot tell at death what his ever-vary-ing future lot will be, as some sin in a former birth may require to be expiated : the true Christian, when dying, knows that his sins are forgiven, and that he will at once enter into *eternal* happiness.

COMPARATIVE EFFECTS.

Hinduism and Christianity may be contrasted by their effects in India and England.

India is one of the poorest countries in the world ; England is one of the richest.

In India only about one in five of the people can read ; in England nearly all are educated.

In India women are kept in ignorance and denied religious instruction ; in England, they are educated, and have the same religious privileges as men.

In India, one caste has sought to be called *Bhúdévas,* gods on earth, while they have tried to degrade others beneath the brutes ; in England all have equal rights.

In India, men worship the works of their own hands, animals, trees, and stones ; in England, the one true God alone is wor-shipped.

In India, no moral instruction is given in Hindu temples, while often there is much to deprave ; in England, public worship has an elevating influence.

In India, Hinduism is the great enemy of reform ; in England, Christianity takes the lead in all real improvement.

CONCLUSION.

Let any thoughtful Hindu compare the two systems, and say which is more in accordance with reason and conducive to the good of the human race. Let him also choose the better way and walk in it.

National feeling should not decide the question. The Indian would be an idiot who urged his countrymen to stick to the national conveyances, palanquins and bullock-carts, and refuse to travel by the "foreign" invention of railways. *What is not* TRUE *is not* PATRIOTIC.

Europeans accepted a religion first made known to them by Asiatics. An Indian poet says : " Do not cling to kith and kindred ; disease born with you will destroy you : the medicine which is in the lofty mountain, not born with you, will expel the disorder."

ENGLISH PUBLICATIONS
FOR
INDIAN READERS.

THE RESPONSIBILITIES OF STUDENTS. 32 pp. ½ Anna.

The Anna Library. 1 Anna each.

Mostly with Numerous Illustrations.

INDIAN FABLES. 48 pp.
PICTURES AND STORIES OF WILD BEASTS. 48 pp.
PICTURES AND STORIES OF BIRDS. 48 pp.
IDOLS OF THE EARTH: ANCIENT AND MODERN. 48 pp.
PICTURE STORIES FROM ENGLISH HISTORY. 48 pp.
PICTURE STORIES OF THE ANCIENT GREEKS. 48 pp.
CHOICE PICTURES AND STORIES. 58 pp.
PICTURES AND STORIES FOR THE YOUNG. 48 pp.
PICTURE FABLES. 48 pp.
ASTRONOMY AND ASTROLOGY. 48 pp.
HISTORY OF THE TRUE INCARNATION.
BUDDHA AND HIS RELIGION.
THE AYAH AND LADY.
STORY OF DR. DUFF, BY A. L. O. E.
THE WONDERFUL HOUSE I LIVE IN.

Miscellaneous.
One Anna each.

SHORT PAPERS FOR SEEKERS AFTER TRUTH. 12mo. 112 pp.
A guide to Religious Inquirers, treating of the Existence of God, Sin, the Need of a Revelation, the leading Doctrines of Christianity, &c.

SHORT PAPERS FOR YOUNG MEN. 12mo. 104 pp.
A Sequel to the foregoing. Hints on General Conduct, the Choice of a Profession, and Success in Life.

THE CHRISTIAN RELIGION. 12mo. 68 pp.
By Professor Fisher of Yale College, United States, contains replies to some of the objections brought against Christianity.

1½ Annas each.

ELEMENTS OF CHRISTIAN TRUTH. 12mo. 71 pp.
By the Rev. Murray Mitchell, author of *Letters to Indian Youth.*

ILLUSTRATED STORIES FROM HISTORY. 4to. 40 pp.
Interesting stories from the history of different countries, with a number of pictures.

STORIES FROM EARLY BRITISH HISTORY. 4to. 40 pp.
An account of the progress of Civilization in early Britain, and how the people became Christians.

STORIES FROM EARLY CHRISTIAN HISTORY. 4to. 28 pp.

TRAVELLING BY LAND, ON SEA, AND THROUGH THE AIR. 4to. 18 pp.

FAMOUS CHILDREN OF LONG AGO. 64 pp. 1½ As.
STORY OF THE FIRST CHRISTIAN MISSIONARY TO EUROPE. 66 pp. 1½ As

2 *Annas each, and upwards.*

BUSHNELL'S CHARACTER OF JESUS. 18mo. 92 pp.
By a good American writer, with notes, by the Rev. T. E. Slater.
PICTURE STORIES OF GREAT MEN. 4to. 48 pp. 2 As.
The Lives of Columbus, Peter the Great, Benjamin Franklin, and James Wat
ARABIA AND ITS PROPHET. 4to. 64 pp. 2½ As.
An account of the Arabs, with descriptions of Jeddah, Mecca, Medina; th
History of Muhammad and the early Khalifs; the Koran, Muslim doctrines, Sect
Prayers, Pilgrimages, &c., with pictures of the Kaaba, Mecca, Medina, &c.
PICTURES OF CHINA AND ITS PEOPLE. 4to. 56 pp. 2½ As.
Extent, History, Manners and Customs of the People ; Schools, Examinations
Industries, Travelling; Language and Literature ; Government; Religions ; Indi
and China compared ; with 64 Illustrations.
EMINENT FRIENDS OF MAN ; OR LIVES OF DISTINGUISHED PHILANTHRO
PISTS. 8vo. 158 pp. 4 As. Post-free, 5 As.
Sketches of Howard, Oberlin, Wilberforce, Buxton, Moore, Montefiore, Livese
Earl of Shaftesbury, Father Damien, and others.
LETTERS TO INDIAN YOUTH ON THE EVIDENCES OF CHRISTIANITY. 12mo
207 pp. 6 As. Post-free, 7 As. New edition, enlarged.
By the Rev. Dr. Murray Mitchell. External and Internal Evidences of Christi
anity; Examination of Popular Hinduism, Vedantism, and Muhammadanism.
THE INDIAN STUDENT'S MANUAL. 12mo. 352 pp. 8As. Post-free, 9 As
Hints on Studies, Examinations, Moral Conduct, Religious Duties, and Suc
cess in Life.
THE INDIAN TEACHER'S MANUAL. 12mo. 325pp. 10As. Post-free, 11 As
Directions about School Management, the teaching of English and the Vernacu
lars, preparing for Examinations, &c. It is also shown how the teacher may ai
Social Reform, and otherwise promote the welfare of the people.

India and England.

PICTORIAL TOUR ROUND INDIA. Royal Quarto. 66 pp. 6 As. Post-free
7½ As.
An imaginary tour round India, with visits to Nepal and Cashmere, describin
the principal cities and other objects of interest. With 78 woodcuts illustrative o
the Himalayas, Calcutta, Benares, Agra, Delhi, Bombay, Madras, &c.
PICTORIAL TOUR ROUND ENGLAND. Royal Quarto. 56 pp. 6 As
Post-free, 7½ As.
Description of the chief places of interest; Public Schools and Universities
English Agriculture and Manufactures; the British Government; Home Life
England an example and warning to India. With 104 woodcuts, and coloure
engraving of the Queen Empress.
SIX MONTHS IN ENGLAND. 12mo. 145 pp. 6 As.
A course of lectures delivered to his countrymen by a Native Clergyman of th
Church Missionary Society, Madras.
PICTURES OF ENGLISH HOME LIFE. 8vo. 80 pp. 2 As. ZENANA SERIES
The object is to give some idea of an English Home. It treats of Houses
Furniture, Servants, Cooking, Food, Amusements, and Training of Children, &c.
with 76 illustrations. Educated Hindus might explain it to their wives.

www.ingramcontent.com/pod-product-compliance
Lightning Source LLC
Chambersburg PA
CBHW022017080426
42733CB00007B/633